DUVALLS
OSHA 1926
Crane Safety
CC
Crane and Derrick Safety
Instructors Manual
2014 Edition

© Copyright 2014. All rights reserved

© Copyright 2014. All rights reserved. Warning: United States Copyright Law and International Treaties prohibit unauthorized publication, distribution and reproduction of the whole, part, portion of this Work. Unauthorized use of this copyright in any form, format, sequence or document may result in severe criminal and civil penalties. Violations of this copyright are investigated by the United States Department of Justice and carry, upon conviction of fines up to $250,000 and five years confinement.

A Ficus Tree Publishing LLC., Educational - Technical Publication

Reminder:

Department of Labor Occupational Safety and Health Administration. 29 CFR Part 1926. [Docket No. OSHA-2007-0066] RIN No. 1218-AC61

Cranes and Derricks in Construction: Underground Construction and Demolition.

Agency: Occupational Safety and Health Administration (OSHA), Labor.

Action: Final rule.

SUMMARY: On August 17, 2012, OSHA issued a notice of proposed rulemaking, as well as a companion direct final rule, that proposed applying the requirements in OSHA's 2010 cranes and derricks construction standard to underground construction work and demolition work. The notice of proposed rulemaking also proposed to correct inadvertent errors in the underground construction and demolition standards. After receiving a comment recommending that OSHA clarify the proposed regulatory text of the demolition standard, OSHA clarified the text and is issuing this final rule to apply the cranes and derricks standard to underground construction work and demolition work.

Date: This final rule is effective May 23, 2013. Petitions for the final rule of this final review are due on June 24, 2013.

Intellectual Property Information:

United States Copyright Law and International Treaties prohibit unauthorized publication, distribution, reprinting, photocopying, of the whole, part, portion of this Work. Unauthorized publication, distribution, reprinting of any part, portion or whole of this document may result in severe criminal and civil penalties. All rights to this Work are reserved. Violations of this copyright are investigated by the United States Department of Justice and carry, upon conviction of fines up to $250,000 and five years confinement.

No part of this publication may be reproduced, distributed, posted, broadcast, digitalized, duplicated, photocopied, or electronically scanned by any means or methods, including, without limitation, optical, mechanical, electronic, photocopying, or recording by or in any information storage system, data information retrieval system or retrieval storage system without prior written permission of the author and publisher. Further, and in addition, purchasers of this document do not have the right or permission to republish, reprint, reproduce, photocopy, scan, digitalize, duplicate, post broadcast any or all of the information contained, thus presented herein, and within this document.

Although the Code of Regulations herein identified as 29 CFR OSHA PART 1926 Subparts **A**, B, **C**, D, E, F, G, H, I, J, K, L, M, N, O, P, Q, R, S, T, U, V, W, X, Y, Z and Subparts CC are published by the United States of America, the creative work of researching, formatting, sequencing, developing, structuring the Work of the materials and information contained herein are subject to United States and International Treaties, copyright laws, codes and agreements.

While every effort has been made to ensure the information contained herein is accurate and complete at the time of publication the possibility of typographic errors, omissions, and/or oversights may exist. No patent liability is assumed with respect to the use of the information and material contained herein. This Work was created for use as a literary and educational study guide series in workbook format. This Work is a educational tool for the research, review, and study aid for and of the material and information presented herein. Thus and therefore, it is not the intent of the author or publisher that this work including the information and material contained herein shall be considered, applied, used as the definitive source for the information and material contained herein. Therefore, neither Ficus Tree Publishing, LLC or the author, nor any person or subsidiary thereof shall be liable for any damages resulting from the use, misuse, or reliance on this publication. In addition, this Work was not created or intended to be a stand-alone source document for the use or misuse by individuals, professional occupations, private or corporate entities or private provider educational entities.

A Ficus Tree Publishing LLC. Quick Notes Page

Copyright Information:

ISBN: **ISBN-13: 978-149603186**
        ISBN-10: 1496036182

Publisher Identification: 19262014-CC-ACSK-ED-1-60-150

Author: Du Vall, James W.

Title: DUVALLS OSHA 1926 Crane and Derrick Safety CC
        Instructors Manual 2014 Edition

A Master Study Guide Series for Instructors providing multiple-choice questions with answers. Created and written for OSHA Part 1926 Subpart §1926.1400 Scope to and including §1926.1406 Assembly/Disassembly—employer procedures—general requirements from 29 CFR OSHA Part 1926 Subpart CC - Cranes and Derricks in Construction as published by the Office of the Federal Register National Archives and Records Administration, August 2010. eCFR—Code of Federal Regulations 1/29/2014.

Source Document: OSHA — Occupational Safety and Health Administration
                    Title: Subpart B — Regulations Relating to Labor
                    Chapter XVII
                    U.S. Government Printing Office
                    U.S. Superintendent of Documents Washington D.C. 204-202-0001
                    http://bookstore.gpo.gov (888-512-1899)
                    e-CFR—Code of Federal Regulations

This publication is intended solely as a study guide-workbook, review and aid to persons engaged in the study and application of Architectural, Engineering and Construction Technology. This Work was not created for nor intended to be considered, used or applied as a stand-alone document for any legal entity, professional, or business enterprise.

Printed in the United States of America

© Copyright 2014. All rights reserved. Warning: United States Copyright Law and International Treaties prohibit unauthorized publication, distribution and reproduction of the whole, part, portion of this Work. Unauthorized use of this copyright in any form, format, sequence or document may result in severe criminal and civil penalties. Violations of this copyright are investigated by the United States Department of Justice and carry, upon conviction of fines up to $250,000 and five years confinement.
A Ficus Tree Publishing LLC., Educational - Technical Publication

A Ficus Tree Publishing LLC. Quick Notes Page

Description

DU VALLS OSHA 1926 CC — Cranes and Derricks in Construction. Instructors Manual 2014 Edition, Subpart CC

§1926.1400 Subpart CC—Cranes and Derricks in Construction

This publication provides information in the manner of multiple-choice questions with answers for OSHA §1926.1400 through and including OSHA §1926.1411 including Table T—Minimum Clearance Distances While Traveling With No Load.

§1926.1400 Scope.

1. "(a) This standard applies to power-operated equipment, when used in construction, that can hoist, lower and horizontally move a suspended load. Such equipment includes, but is not limited to: Articulating cranes (such as knuckle-boom cranes); crawler cranes; floating cranes; cranes on barges; locomotive cranes; mobile cranes (such as wheel-mounted, rough-terrain, all-terrain, commercial truck-mounted, and boom truck cranes); multi-purpose machines when configured to hoist and lower (by means of a winch or hook) and horizontally move a suspended load; industrial cranes (such as carry-deck cranes); dedicated pile drivers; service/mechanic trucks with a hoisting device; a crane on a monorail; tower cranes (such as a fixed jib, *i.e.*, "hammerhead boom"), luffing boom and self-erecting); pedestal cranes; portal cranes; overhead gantry cranes; sideboom cranes; derricks; and variations of such equipment. However, items listed in paragraph (c) of this section are excluded from the scope of this standard."

The entire paragraph above is taken as a verbatim presentation from the lead-in paragraph for OSHA standard **§1926.1400 Subpart CC—Cranes and Derricks in Construction**. What we have accomplished with the creation of DUVALLS OSHA 1926 CC Instructors Manual 2014 Edition is the dissection of this entire statement into a series of multiple-choice test type questions presented in convenient, easy to read, easy to follow test type questions. All questions are provided with answers, all questions with their answers are written in the specific sequential format of the United States Department of Labor publication.

For convenience of study and research each work presented by Ficus Tree Publishing LLC., for OSHA is generally limited from 60 to 150 pages plus or minus.

The Instructor, the student, the researcher will generally encounter little difficulty when reading, studying, and researching the difficult Federal Laws, Rules and Regulations (CFR's) of our complex but very important OSHA—Occupational Safety and Health Act when presented in this modern method study format.

This work is printed and marketed through and by Amazon/Create Space. Soon to be available on Kindle.

§1926 Subpart CC—Cranes and Derricks in Construction

OSHA 1926 Subpart CC—Cranes and Derricks in Construction. Authority: 40 U.S.C. 3701; 29 U.S.C. 653, 655, 657; and Secretary of Labor's Order No. 5-2007 (72 FR31159, or 1-2012 (77 FR 3912), as applicable; and 29CFR part 1911.

This Work provides 15 test sets for OSHA standards 1926.1400 to and including 1926.1411. In approximately 150 pages and over 400 multiple-choice, test type questions with answers.

A brief description of the information contained within this Instructors Manual: The tests; The tests are designed to enable Instructors and lecturers to focus on the development of the course Semester, Quarter syllabus by providing complete and up to date information for and of Part 1926 Subpart CC—Cranes and Derricks in Construction. The test series will generally follow the exacting published format of the standards provided by the Department of Labor in electronic and hard copy editions of this stated OSHA Part. Detailed work available to Instructors includes specific multiple-choice questions with answers for the following:

§1926.1400 Scope; §1926.1401 Definitions; §1926.1402 Ground conditions; §1926.1403 Assembly/Disassembly—selection of manufacturer or employer procedures; §1926.1404 Assembly/Disassembly—general requirements (applies to all assembly and disassembly operations). §1926.405 Disassembly—additional requirements for dismantling of booms and jibs (applies to both the use of manufacturer procedures and employer procedures). §1926.1406 Assembly/Disassembly—employer procedures—general requirements. §1926.1407 Power line safety (up to 350 kV) and §1926.1408 Power line safety (up to 350 kV—equipment operations concludes with Table T—Minimum Clearance Distances While traveling With no Load.

The second and following section of DUVALLS OSHA 1926 Subpart CC—Cranes and Derricks in Construction commences with the equally important §1926.1412 Inspections. This test series is presently under review and updating.

Contents Subpart CC Tests

Title: Page 1

Docket reminder: Page 2

Intellectual Property Information: Page 3

Copyright Information: Page 5

Description: Page 7

Contents. Page 9

The OSHA Text
Multiple-choice questions with answers

Test CC-1 §1926.1400 Scope. Page 13

Test CC-2 §1926.1401 Definitions. Page 23

Test CC-3 §1926.1401 Definitions. Page 37

Test CC-4 §1926.1401 Definitions. Page 51

Test CC-5 §1926.1402 Ground Conditions. Page 57

Test CC-6 §1926.1403 Assembly/Disassembly—
Selection of manufacturer or employer procedures. Page 61

Test CC-7 §1926.1404 Assembly/Disassembly—general requirements. Page 63

Test CC-8 §1926.1405 Disassembly—Additional requirements for dismantling of booms and jibs
(applies to both the use of manufacturer and employer procedures). Page 81

Test CC-9 §1926.1406 Assembly/Disassembly—
Employer procedures—general requirements. Page 83

Test CC-10 §1926.1407 Power line safety (up to 350 kV) —
Assembly and Disassembly. Page 85

Test CC-11 §1926.1408 Power line safety (up to 350 kV)—
Equipment operations. Page 93

Contents Subpart CC Tests (continued)

Test CC-13 §1926.1409 Power line safety (over 350 kV). Page 115

Test CC-14 §1926.1410 Power line safety (all voltages)—
Equipment operations closer than the table A zone. Page 117

Test CC-15 §1926.1411 Power line safety—
While traveling under or near power lines with no load. Page 139

OSHA Part 1926 Subpart CC
Cranes and Derricks in Construction
Crane and Derrick Safety Series

From Regulations (Standards - 29 CFR) - Table of Contents § 1926.1400
Authority: 40 U.S.C. 3701; 29 U.S.C. 653, 655, 657; and Secretary of Labor's Order No. 5-2007 (72 FR 31159) or 1-2012 (77 FR 3912), as applicable; and 29 CFR part 1911.
Source: 75 FR 48135, Aug. 9, 2010, unless otherwise noted.

1926 Safety and Health Regulations For Construction, Subpart CC - Cranes and Derricks in Construction. Authority for 1926 Subpart CC. Authority: Section 3704 of the Contract Work Hours and Safety Standards Act (40 U.S.C. 3701) sections 4, 6, and 8 of the Occupational Safety and Health Act of 1970 (29 U.S.C. 653, 655, 657); Secretary of Labor's Order No. 5-2007 (72 FR 311159) and 29 CFR part 1911. [75 FR 48135, Aug. 9, 2010]

For additional information: http://www.osha.gov/
Telephone 800-321-OSHA (6742) TTY:877-889-5627

When Government publications, manuals or similar bound publication become available from the United States Government Printing Office and/or publications from independent private printing sources such document may be expected to become suggested or mandatory for all testing protocols.

Suggested Key Words and Vocabulary from OSHA Part 1926 — Subpart CC

Key Words from 1926 Subpart CC: Roustabout • power-operated equipment • knuckle-boom crane • crawler cranes • floating cranes • cranes on barges • locomotive cranes • mobile cranes • wheel-mounted cranes • rough terrain cranes • all-terrain cranes • commercial-truck mounted cranes • boom truck cranes • multi-purpose machines • winch • hook • industrial cranes • carry-deck cranes • dedicated pile drivers • service/mechanic truck mounted cranes • monorail cranes • magnet cranes • tower cranes • Chicago boom cranes • Articulating cranes • fixed jib cranes • hammerhead cranes • lufting boom cranes • self-erecting cranes • pedestal cranes • portal cranes • overhead cranes • gantry cranes • straddle cranes • sideboom cranes • derricks • Power shovels • Automotive wreckers • wheel loaders • excavators • backhoes • draglines • track loaders • rigging • digger derricks • auguring • vehicle-mounted aerial devices • self-propelled elevating work platforms • telescopic/hydraulic gantry systems • stacker cranes • self-propelled cranes • chainfall • dedicated drilling rigs • powered industrial trucks • forklifts • helicopter cranes • gin poles • dredge-related operations • precast concrete members • panels • roof trusses • wooden • metal • cold-formed • steel • prefabricated • building sections • steel-decking • beams • columns • metal buildings • systems-engineered • structural steel member

A Ficus Tree Publishing LLC. Quick Notes Page

DU VALLS
OSHA 1926 Subpart CC — Cranes and Derricks in Construction
OSHA 1926.1400 Scope
Instructors Manual 2014 Edition
OSHA Test CC - 1

§1926.1400 Scope.

1. This standard applies to power-operated equipment, when used in construction, that can hoist, lower and horizontally move a suspended load. From section § ____.
   - (a) 1926.1400
   - (b) 1926.1400(a)
   - (c) 1926.1400(b)
   - (d) 1926.1400(c)

   Answer: (b) 1926.1400(a) Scope. Subpart CC

§1926.1400(a)

2. Such equipment includes, but is not limited to: ___ cranes (such as knuckle-boom cranes); crawler cranes,; floating cranes; cranes on barges; locomotive cranes; mobile cranes(such as wheel-mounted, rough terrain, all-terrain, commercial truck-mounted, boom truck cranes); multi-purpose machines when configured to hoist and lower (by means of a winch or hook) and horizontally move a suspended load; industrial cranes (such as carry-deck cranes); dedicated pile drivers; service/mechanic trucks with a hoisting device; a crane on a monorail; tower cranes (such as fixed jib, *i.e.* "hammerhead boom"), lufting boom and self-erecting); pedestal cranes; portal cranes; overhead and gantry cranes; straddle cranes; sideboom cranes; derricks; and variations of such equipment.
   - (a) Construction
   - (b) Electrical
   - (c) Power -driven
   - (d) Articulating

   Answer: (d) Articulating. § 1926.1400(a) Subpart CC

§1926.1400(a)

3. However, items listed in paragraph ___ of this section are excluded from the scope of this standard. From ___.
   - (a) (a)
   - (b) (b)
   - (c) (c)
   - (d) (d)

   Answer: (c) 1926.1400(a). Subpart CC

Crane and Derrick Safety - Subpart CC

§1926.1400(b)
4. Attachments: This standard applies to equipment included in paragraph (a) of this section when used with ___.
   - (a) accessories
   - (b) attachments
   - (c) modifications
   - (d) all equipment

   Answer: (b) attachments. § 1926.1400(b) Subpart CC

§1926.1400(c)
5. Such attachments, whether crane-attached or suspended include, but are not limited to: Hooks, ___, grapples, clamshell buckets, , ___ buckets, concrete buckets, drag lines, personnel platforms, augers or drill and pile driving equipment.
   - (a) magnets, lemon peel
   - (b) horse shoe magnets, grapefruit peel
   - (c) magnets, orange peel
   - (d) rivet-able, lemon-peel

   Answer: (c) magnets, orange peel. § 1926.1400(c) Subpart CC

§1926.1400(c)
6. 1926.1400(c) addresses ___.
   - (a) Attachments
   - (b) Accessories
   - (c) Exclusions
   - (d) Modifications

   Answer: (c) Exclusions. §1926.1400(c) Subpart CC

§1926.1400(c)(1)
7. This standard does not cover: (1) Machinery included in paragraph (a) while it has been converted or adapted for an non-hoisting/lifting use. Such conversions /adaptations include, but are not limited to, power shovels, excavators, and ___.
   - (a) concrete pumps
   - (b) lift stations
   - (c) hydraulic pumps
   - (d) thrust blocks

   Answer: (a) concrete pumps § 1926.1400(c)(1) Subpart CC

§1926.1400(c)(2)
8. This standard does not cover: (2) Power shovels, excavators, ___, backhoes, loader backhoes, track loaders.
   - (a) front end loaders
   - (b) wheel loaders
   - (c) multi-position tractors
   - (d) hay lifters

   Answer: (b) wheel loaders §1926.1400(c) and § 1926.1400(c)(2) Subpart CC

Crane and Derrick Safety - Subpart CC

§1926.1400(c)(2)
9. This machinery is also excluded when used with chains, slings, or other rigging to lift ___ loads.
   (a) dangerous
   (b) heavy
   (c) light
   (d) suspended
   Answer: (d) suspended § 1926.1400(c)(2) Subpart CC

§1926.1400 (c)(3)
10. This subpart does not cover: Automotive wreckers and tow trucks when used to ___ and haul vehicles.
    (a) transport persons
    (b) pull
    (c) move vehicles
    (d) clear wrecks
    Answer: (d) clear wrecks §1926.1400(3) Subpart CC

§1926.1400 (c)(4)
11. This subpart does not cover; Digger derricks when used for augering holes for poles carrying electric or telecommunication lines, placing and removing the poles, and for handling ___ materials to be installed on or removed from the poles.
    (a) insulators
    (b) electrical
    (c) associated
    (d) crossarms
    Answer: (c) associated §1926.1400(c)(4) Subpart CC

§1926.1400 (c)(4)
12. Digger derricks used in work subject to 29 CFR part 1926, subpart V, must comply with §1910.___.
    (a) 260(g)(7)
    (b) 268(s)(40)
    (c) 269(m)(17)
    (d) 271(r)(9)
    Answer: (b) 268(s)(40). §1926.1400(c)(4) Subpart CC

§1926.1400 (c)(4)
13. Digger derricks used in construction work for telecommunication service (as defined at §1910.___) must comply with all the provisions of §1910.___.
    (a) 268(s)(40), 268
    (b) 269 (m) (17), 269
    (c) 271 (r)(9), 271
    (d) 273.2331(s)(23), 273
    Answer: (a) 268(s)(40), 268. §1926.1400(c)(4) Subpart CC

Crane and Derrick Safety - Subpart CC

§1926.1400 (c)(5)
14.   This subpart does not cover: Machinery originally designed as vehicle-mounted aerial devices (for lifting personnel) and ___ elevating work platforms.
   (a)   self-propelled
   (b)   gasoline propelled
   (c)   battery propelled
   (d)   diesel propelled
   Answer: (a) self-propelled § 1926.1400(c)(5) Subpart CC

§1926.1400 (c)(6)
15.   1926.1400(c)(6) discusses ___.
   (a)   Battery propelled elevating work platforms
   (b)   Self-propelled elevating work platforms
   (c)   Telescopic/hydraulic gantry systems
   (d)   Servicing of overhead cranes
   Answer: (c) Telescopic/hydraulic gantry systems §1926.1400(c)(6) Subpart CC

§1926.1400 (c)(7)
16.   1926.1400(c)(7) mentions ___.
   (a)   Stacker cranes
   (b)   Stacker derricks
   (c)   Deep well injection systems
   (d)   Lift stations
   Answer: (a) Stacker cranes. §1926.1400(c)(7) Subpart CC

§1926.1400 (c)(8)
17.   This subpart does not cover: Powered industrial trucks (forklifts), except when configured to hoist and lower (by means of a winch or hook) and ___ move a suspended load.
   (a)   vertically
   (b)   horizontally
   (c)   laterally
   (d)   diagonally
   Answer: (b) horizontally. § 1926.1400(c)(8) Subpart CC

§1926.1400 (c)(9)
18.   This subpart does not cover: Mechanic's trucks with a hoisting device when related to ___ maintenance and repair.
   (a)   vehicle
   (b)   truck
   (c)   hoist
   (d)   equipment
   Answer: (d) equipment. § 1926.1400(c)(9) Subpart CC

Crane and Derrick Safety - Subpart CC

§1926.1400 (c)(10)
19. This subpart does not cover: Machinery that hoists by using a come-a-long or ___.
    (a) ball and chain
    (b) tow line
    (c) chainfall
    (d) block and tackle
    Answer: (c) chainfall § 1926.1400(c)(10) Subpart CC

§1926.1400 (c)(11)
20. 1926.1400(c)(11) discusses ___.
    (a) Dedicated drilling rigs
    (b) Anchor handling
    (c) Material delivery
    (d) Roustabouts
    Answer: (a) Dedicated drilling rigs. § 1926.1400(c)(11) Subpart CC

§1926.1400 (c)(12)
21. 1926.1400(c)(12) states this subpart does not cover ___.
    (a) Helicopter cranes
    (b) Tree trimming
    (c) Gin poles when used for the erection of communication towers
    (d) Drilling rigs
    Answer: (c) Gin poles when used for the erection of communication towers § 1926.1400(c)(12) Subpart CC

§1926.1400 (c)(13)
22. 1926.1400(c)(13) states this subpart does not cover ___.
    (a) Tree trimming and tree removal work
    (b) Helicopter Cranes
    (c) Material delivery
    (d) Roustabouts
    Answer: (a) Tree trimming and tree removal work § 1926.1400 (c)(13) Subpart CC

§1926.1400 (c)(14)
23. This subpart does not cover: Anchor handling or dredge-related operations with a vessel or barge using an affixed ____.
    (a) Pile driver
    (b) A-frame
    (c) Gantry
    (d) Overhead crane
    Answer: (b) A-frame § 1926.1400(c)(14) Subpart AA

Crane and Derrick Safety - Subpart CC

§1926.1400 (c)(15)
24. Roustabouts, laborers on oil rigs, derricks, cranes are not covered under 1926.1400(c)____.
 (a) 14
 (b) 15
 (c) 16
 (d) 17
 Answer: (b) 15. §1926.1400(c)(15) Subpart AA

§1926.1400 (c)(16)
25. Helicopter cranes are not covered by §1926.1400(c)____.
 (a) 14
 (b) 15
 (c) 16
 (d) 17
 Answer: (c) 16. §1926.1400(c)(16) Subpart AA

§1926.1400 (c)(17)
26. 1926.1400(c)(17) discusses ___.
 (a) Material delivery
 (b) Floating cranes
 (c) Oil derricks
 (d) Deep well injection systems
 Answer: (a) Material delivery §1926.1400(c)(17) Subpart AA

§1926.1400 (i)
27. Articulating/knuckle-boom truck cranes that deliver materials to a construction site when used to building transfer materials from the truck crane to the ground, without ___ sequence for hoisting. Are not covered by this paragraph.
 (a) connecting directly for lifting onto or into the job site
 (b) arranging the materials in a particular
 (c) becoming a member of the rigging process team
 (d) directly participating in the hoisting and lifting of the project
 Answer: (b) arranging the materials in a particular §1926.1400(c)(17)(i) Subpart CC

§1926.1400 (ii)
28. This subpart does not cover: Articulating/knuckle-boom truck cranes that deliver material to a construction site when the crane is used to transfer building supply sheet goods or building supply packaged materials from the truck crane onto a structure, using a ___ at the end of the boom, but only when the truck crane is equipped with a properly functioning automatic ___ device.
 (a) fork/cradle, hoist
 (b) overload prevention, hoist
 (c) fork/cradle, overload prevention
 (d) hook or sling, unloading
 Answer: (c) fork/cradle, overload prevention. §1926.1400(c)(17(ii) Subpart CC

Crane and Derrick Safety - Subpart CC

§1926.1400 (ii)
29. Such sheet goods or packaged materials include, but are not limited to: Sheets of sheet rock, sheets of plywood, bags of cement, sheets or packages of roofing shingles, and ____.
    (a) roofing nails
    (b) and rolls of roofing felt
    (c) tar kettles and roofing tools
    (d) tar kettles and roofing equipment
    Answer: (b) and rolls of roofing felt §1926.1400(c)(17)(ii) Subpart CC

§1926.1400 (iii)
30. 1926.1400(c)(17)(iii) states ___.
    (a) This exclusion does not apply when:
    (b) This exclusion does not apply for:
    (c) This exclusion does not apply whenever:
    (d) This exclusion does not apply:
    Answer: (a) This exclusion does not apply when: § 1926.1400(c)(17)(iii) Subpart CC

§1926.1400 (iii)
31. This exclusion does not apply when: The articulating/knuckle boom crane is used to hold, support or ___ the material to facilitate a construction activity, such as holding a material in place while it is attached to the structure.
    (a) install
    (b) place
    (c) stabilize
    (d) attach
    Answer: (c) stabilize § 1926.1400(c)(17)(iii)(A) Subpart CC

§1926.1400 (iii)
32. According to OSHA Part 1926.1400(c)(17)(iii)(B): This exclusion does not apply when: The material being handled by the articulating/knuckle boom cranes is a ___ component.
    (a) manufactured
    (b) precast
    (c) prestressed
    (d) prefabricated
    Answer: (d) prefabricated. §1926.1400(c)(17)(iii)(B) Subpart CC

§1926.1400 (iii)
33. According to OSHA Part 1926.1400(c)(17)(iii)(B): Such prefabricated units include, but are not limited to: Precast concrete members or panels, roof trusses, (wooded, cold-formed metal, steel, or other material), prefabricated building sections such as, but not limited to: Floor panels, wall panels, roof panels, roof ___, or similar items;
    (a) assemblies
    (b) systems
    (c) structures
    (d) cupolas
    Answer: (c) structures §1926.1400(c)(17)(iii)(B) Subpart CC

Crane and Derrick Safety - Subpart CC

§1926.1400 (iii)

34. According to OSHA Part 1926.1400(c)(17)(iii)(C): This exclusion does not apply when: The material being handled by the crane is a structural steel member (for example, steel joists, beams, columns, ___(bundled or unbundled) or a component of a ___ metal building (as defined in 29 CFR 1926 subpart R).
    (a) steel-decking, systems-engineered
    (b) reinforcing steel, engineered
    (c) structural steel, systems-engineered
    (d) post-tensioned steel decking, systems-engineered
    Answer: (a) steel decking, systems-engineered. §1926.1400(c)(17)(iii)(C) Subpart CC

§1926.1400 (iii)

35. 29 CFR OSHA Part 1926.1400(c)(17)(iii)(D) states:
    (a) This activity is specifically excluded under § 1400(c)(17)(i) and (ii)
    (b) This activity is not specifically excluded under § 1400(c)(17)(i) and (ii)
    (c) This activity shall be specifically excluded under § 1400(c)(17)(i) and (ii)
    (d) This activity shall not be specifically excluded under § 1400(c)(17)(i) and (ii)
    Answer: (b) This activity is not specifically excluded under § 1400(c)(17)(i) and (ii) § 1926.1400(c)(17)(iii)(D) Subpart CC

§1926.1400 (iii)

36. According to 29 CFR OSHA Part 1926 Subpart 1926.1400(d). All sections of this subpart CC apply to the equipment covered in this standard unless___.
    (a) specifically forbidden
    (b) specifically prohibited
    (c) specifically approved
    (d) specified otherwise
    Answer: (d) specified otherwise. §1926.1400(d) Subpart CC

§1926.1400 (iii)

37. 29 CFR OSHA Part 1926.1400(e) states: The duties of controlling entities under this subpart include, but are not limited to the duties specified in §1926.1402(c), § 1926.1402(e) and ___.
    (a) § 1926.1402(f)
    (b) § 1926.1402(g)
    (c) § 1926.1412(a)
    (d) § 1926.1424(b)
    Answer: (d) §1926.1424(b). §1926.1400(e) Subpart CC

Crane and Derrick Safety - Subpart CC

§1926.1400 (iii)
38. Where provisions of this standard direct an operator, crewmember, or other employees to take certain actions, the employer must establish, ___ communicate to the ___ persons, and enforce, work rules to ensure compliance with such ___.
    (a)   training procedures to, designated, requirements
    (b)   effectively, relevant, provisions
    (c)   directly, designated, provisions
    (d)   effectively, qualified, procedures
    Answer: (b) effectively, relevant, provisions §1926.1400(f) Subpart CC

§1926.1400 (iii)
39. For work covered by subpart V of this part, compliance with 29 CFR § 1910.269 (p) is deemed compliance with §1926.1407 through 1926.____.
    (a)   1409
    (b)   1410
    (c)   1411
    (d)   1412
    Answer: (c) 1411 § 1926.1400(g) Subpart CC

§1926.1400 (iii)
40. Section 1926.1402 does not apply to cranes designed for use on railroad tracks, when used on railroad tracks that are part of the general railroad system of transportation that is regulated pursuant to the Federal Railroad Administration under ___, and that comply with the applicable Federal Railroad Administration requirements §1926.1402(f).
    (a)   49 CFR part 211
    (b)   49 CFR part 213
    (c)   49 CFR part 215
    (d)   49 CFR part 217
    Answer: Answer: (b) 49 CFR Part 213 § 1926.1400(h) Subpart CC

[75 FR 48135, Aug. 9, 2010, as amended at 78 FR 32116, May 29, 2013]

A Ficus Tree Publishing LLC. Quick Notes Page

DU VALLS
OSHA 1926 Subpart CC — Cranes and Derricks in Construction
OSHA 1926.1401 Definitions
Instructors Manual 2014 Edition
OSHA Test CC - 2

1926.1401 Definitions

The next section of 29 CFR OSHA Part 1926.1401 Definitions, Subpart CC requires careful reading of words, language, nomenclature that generally appear is isolated questions on multiple-choice college format tests. The statement college format does not state or imply the questions are only for college level students. Rather, the term describes the type of test provided by the professor, teacher, instructor or lecturer that is suitable for lecture and study purposes.

1926.1401 is important for the content of the material. With each subpart of it is the practice of OSHA to provide a listing of definitions as a necessity of adequately describing legal terms in courtroom settings. Always, know where the definitions are located in each subpart. If possible a small easily identified tab should be used to assist in the quick location of the definitions. This, 29 CFR OSHA Part 1926 Subpart CC is an important part of the Department of Labor documents.

OSHA 1926 Cranes and Derricks in Construction, Standard number 1926.1401. Definitions.

§1926.1401 Definitions
1. An individual who meets this subpart's requirements for an A/D director, irrespective of the person's formal job title or whether the person is non-management or management personnel is defined by this subpart as: ___.
    (a) A/C director
    (b) A/M director
    (c) A/D director
    (d) A/T director
    Answer: (c) A/D director (assembly/disassembly director) § 1926.1401 Subpart CC Definitions

§1926.1401 Definitions
2. Articulating crane means a a crane whose boom consists of a series of ___, pin connected structural members, typically manipulated to extend or retract by power from hydraulic cylinders.
    (a) flexible
    (b) collapsing
    (c) folding
    (d) rigid
    Answer: (c) folding (for homework go to the Internet to locate a picture or pictorial of an Articulating crane) § 1926.1401 Subpart CC Definitions

Crane and Derrick Safety - Subpart CC

§1926.1401 Definitions

3. Assembly/Disassembly means the assembly and or disassembly of equipment covered under this standard. With regard to tower cranes, "____" replaces the term "____" and "____" replaces the term "____".
   (a) elevated, assembly, lowered, disassembly
   (b) erecting and climbing, assembly, dismantling, disassembly
   (c) erecting, assembly, lowering, dismantling
   (d) climbing, assembly, dismantling, disassembly
   Answer: (b) erecting and climbing, assembly, dismantling, disassembly § 1926.1401 Subpart CC Definitions

§1926.1401 Definitions

4. Regardless of whether the crane is initially erected to its full height or is climbed in stages, the process of increasing the height of the crane is an ___ process.
   (a) erection
   (b) assembly
   (c) elevating
   (d) climbing
   Answer: (a) erection § 1926.1401 Definitions Subpart CC

§1926.1401 Definitions

5. Assist crane means a crane used to ___ in assembling or disassembling a crane.
   (a) expedite
   (b) assist
   (c) support
   (d) aid employees
   Answer: (b) assist § 1926.1401 Definitions Subpart CC

§1926.1401 Definitions

6. Attachments means any device that ___ the range of tasks that can be done by the equipment. Examples include, but are not limited to: An auger, drill, magnet, pile-driver, and boom attached platform.
   (a) increases
   (b) develops
   (c) expands
   (d) modifies
   Answer: (c) expands § 1926.1401 Definitions Subpart CC

§1926.1401 Definitions

7. A signal made by a distinct sound or series of sounds is defined as ____.
   (a) Audible sound
   (b) Audible signal
   (c) Alarm signal
   (d) Signal alarm
   Answer: (b) Audible signal § 1926.1401 Definitions Subpart CC

Crane and Derrick Safety - Subpart CC

§1926.1401 Definitions
8. According to OSHA Part 1926 Subpart CC - Signals, include, but are not limited to sounds made by a bell, horn or ___.
   - (a) audible alarm
   - (b) audible signal
   - (c) gong
   - (d) whistle

   Answer: (d) whistle § 1926.1401 Definitions Subpart CC

§1926.1401 Definitions
9. Blocking is also referred to as ___.
   - (a) barricading
   - (b) cribbing
   - (c) braking
   - (d) stopping

   Answer: (b) cribbing § 1926.1401 Definitions Subpart CC

§1926.1401 Definitions
10. Wood or other material used to support equipment or a component and distribute loads to the ground is defined in §1926.1401 Definitions as: ___.
    - (a) Cribbed
    - (b) Blocking
    - (c) Cribbing
    - (d) Timbers

    Answer: (b) Blocking, § 1926.1401 Definitions Subpart CC

§1926.1401 Definitions
11. Blocking is typically used to support ___ boom sections during assembly/disassembly and under outrigger and stabilizer floats.
    - (a) crane
    - (b) derrick
    - (c) lattice
    - (d) elevated

    Answer: (c) lattice § 1926.1401 Definitions - second sentence Subpart CC

§1926.1401 Definitions
12. A single-point adjustable suspension scaffold consisting of a seat or sling (which may be incorporated into a full body harness) designed to support one employee in a sitting position is defined by 1926.1401 Definitions as a ___.
    - (a) Scaffold
    - (b) Working chair
    - (c) Boatswain's chair
    - (d) Captain's chair

    Answer: (c) Boatswain's chair § 1926.1401 Definitions Subpart CC

Crane and Derrick Safety - Subpart CC

§1926.1401 Definitions
13. Bogie means, as defined by this subpart ___.
    (a) the suspension tensioning wheel system of tracked vehicles
    (b) the nick-name of a well known late Hollywood actor
    (c) an evil spirit known as the Boogieman
    (d) a term associated with tower cranes in this subpart
    Answer: (d) a term associated with tower cranes in this subpart. See "travel bogie," which is defined below. §1926.1401 Definitions Subpart CC

§1926.1401 Definitions
14. An inclined spar, strut, or other long structural member which supports the upper hoisting tackle on a crane or derrick is defined by OSHA Part 1926 Subpart CC as a ___.
    (a) Beam
    (b) Guy
    (c) Boom
    (d) Truss
    Answer: (c) Boom § 1926.1401 Definitions Subpart CC

§1926.1401 Definitions
15. Typically, the length and vertical angle of the boom can be ___ to achieve increased height or height and reach when lifting loads.
    (a) varied
    (b) changed
    (c) modified
    (d) altered
    Answer: (a) varied § 1926.1401 Definitions Subpart CC

§1926.1401 Definitions
16. According to 29 CFR OSHA Part 1926 Subpart CC: Booms can usually be grouped into general categories of hydraulically extendable, ___ type, latticed section, cable supported type or articulating type.
    (a) sleeve
    (b) cantilevered
    (c) I - beam
    (d) geodesic
    Answer: (b) cantilevered § 1926.1401 Definitions Subpart CC

§1926.1401 Definitions
17. 29 CFR OSHA Part 1926.1401 Definitions, describes ___ types of crane booms.
    (a) 4
    (b) 5
    (c) 6
    (d) 7
    Answer: (b) 5 § 1926.1401 Definitions Subpart CC

Crane and Derrick Safety - Subpart CC

§1926.1401 Definitions
18. On tower cranes, if the "boom" (*i.e.*, principal horizontal structure) is fixed, it is referred to as a ____; if it is movable up and down, it is referred to as a ____.
    (a)   boom, cantilever
    (b)   cantilever, boom
    (c)   boom, jib
    (d)   jib, boom
Answer: (d) jib, boom § 1926.1401 Definitions Subpart CC

§1926.1401 Definitions
19. A device which measures the angle of the boom relative to horizontal is called a ___.
    (a)   Boom angle indicator
    (b)   Angle indicator
    (c)   Angle setting indicator
    (d)   Boom angle and setting indicator
Answer: (a) Boom angle indicator § 1926.1401 Definitions Subpart CC

§1926.1401 Definitions
20. *Boom hoist limiting device* includes boom hoist disengaging device, boom hoist shut-off, boom hoist disconnect, boom hoist *relief*, boom hoist ___, automatic boom stop device, or derrick limiter.
    (a)   emergency stop
    (b)   kick-out
    (c)   block
    (d)   emergency release
Answer: (b) kick-out §1926.1401 Definitions Subpart CC

§1926.1401 Definitions
21. The type of device that disengages boom hoist power when the boom reaches a predetermined operating angle is defined by 29 CFR OSHA Part 1926 Definitions Subpart CC Cranes and Derricks in Construction as a ___.
    (a)   *Boom hoist override control switch*
    (b)   *Boom hoist limiting device*
    (c)   *Boom hoist relief*
    (d)   *Boom hoist operating angle kick-off device*
Answer: (b) *Boom hoist limiting device* § 1926.1401 Definitions Subpart CC

§1926.1401 Definitions
22. The device that also sets brakes or closes valves to prevent the boom from lowering after power is disengaged is defined by OSHA Part 1926.1401 Definitions as a ___.
    (a)   *Boom hoist limiting device*
    (b)   *Boom hoist hydraulic safety control*
    (c)   *Boom hoist hydraulic safety device*
    (d)   *Boom hoist power control*
Answer: (a) *Boom hoist limiting device* § 1926.1401 Definitions Subpart CC

Crane and Derrick Safety - Subpart CC

§1926.1401 Definitions
23. The length of the permanent part of the boom (such as ruled markings on the boom) or, as in some computerized systems, the length of the boom with extensions/attachments is defined by 29 CFR OSHA Part 1926.1401 Definitions as the ___.
    (a) *Boom hoist limiting device*
    (b) *Boom hoist length controller*
    (c) *Boom length indicator*
    (d) *Boom length indicator limiting device*
    Answer: (c) *Boom length indicator* § 1926.1401 Definitions Subpart CC

§1926.1401 Definitions
24. *Boom stop* includes boom stops, (belly straps with struts/standoff), telescoping boom stops, attachment boom stops, and ___.
    (a) backstops
    (b) shortstops
    (c) blocking stops
    (d) safety stops
    Answer: (a) backstops § 1926.1401 Definitions Subpart CC

§1926.1401 Definitions
25. Devices that restrict the boom from moving above a certain maximum angle and toppling over backward are defined by 29 CFR OSHA Part 1926.1401 Subpart CC as ___.
    (a) Hoist limiting devices
    (b) Backstops
    (c) Safety stops
    (d) Boom stops
    Answer: (d) Boom stops (second sentence) § 1926.1401 Definitions Subpart CC

§1926.1401 Definitions
26. *Boom suspension system* means a systems of pendants, running ropes, ___, and other hardware which supports the boom tip and controls the boom angle.
    (a) steel cables
    (b) steel ropes
    (c) shiv's
    (d) sheaves
    Answer: (d) sheaves § 1926.1401 Definitions Subpart CC

§1926.1401 Definitions
27. As defined by 29 CFR OSHA Part 1926 Definitions Subpart CC: Builder means ___.
    (a) the General Contractor of the project
    (b) a General Contractor or a Residential Contractor
    (c) the builder/constructor of equipment
    (d) the current project under construction
    Answer: (c) the builder/constructor of equipment § 1926.1401 Definitions Subpart CC

Crane and Derrick Safety - Subpart CC

§1926.1401 Definitions

28. If you could put a support under that point, you could balance the object on the support. This is a descriptive statement in 29 CFR OSHA Part 1926 Definitions Subpart CC for: ___.
    (a) The load point
    (b) The lifting point
    (c) Center of Gravity
    (d) Moment
    Answer: (c) Center of Gravity § 1926.1401 Definitions - Center of Gravity Subpart CC

§1926.1401 Definitions

29. *The center of gravity of any object* is the ____ in the object around which its weight is evenly distributed.
    (a) axis
    (b) point
    (c) central point
    (d) geometric center
    Answer: (b) point § 1926.1401 Definitions Subpart CC

§1926.1401 Definitions

30. A welder who meets nationally recognized certification requirements applicable to the task being performed. Is defined by 29 CRF OSHA Part 1926 Definitions as a ___.
    (a) Qualified welder
    (b) Certified
    (c) Certified welder
    (d) Welder
    Answer: (c) Certified welder § 1926.1401 Definitions Subpart CC

§1926.1401 Definitions

31. The process in which a tower crane is raised to a new working height is defined by 29 CFR OSHA Part 1926.1401 as ____.
    (a) Raising
    (b) Climbing
    (c) Running
    (d) Extending
    Answer: (b) Climbing § 1926.1401 Definitions Subpart CC

§1926.1401 Definitions

32. There are two methods used to elevate or increase the height of tower cranes. The two methods used are either by adding additional tower sections to the top of the crane (___), or by a system in which then entire crane is raised inside the structure (___).
    (a) topping, slipping
    (b) top climbing, inside climbing
    (c) top structuring, inside structuring
    (d) top building, inside building
    Answer: (b) top climbing, inside climbing § 1401 Definitions Subpart CC

Crane and Derrick Safety - Subpart CC

§1926.1401 Definitions
33. A mechanical device typically consisting of a chain or cable attached at each end that is used to facilitate movement of materials through leverage is defined by 29 CFR OSHA Part 1926.1401 Definitions as a:
    (a) *Come-a-long*
    (b) *Pulley-and-hook*
    (c) *Chain hoist*
    (d) *Fulcrum*
    Answer: (a) *Come-a-long* § 1026.1401 Definitions Subpart CC

§1926.1401 Definitions
34. One, who is capable of identifying existing and predictable hazards in the surroundings or working conditions which are unsanitary, hazardous, or dangerous to employees, and who has the authorization to take prompt corrective measures to eliminate them. Is defined by §1926.1401 Definitions as a: ___.
    (a) *Safety engineer*
    (b) *Safety inspector*
    (c) *Competent person*
    (d) *Project supervisor*
    Answer: (c) Competent person § 1926.1401 Definitions Subpart CC

§1926.1401 Definitions
35. *Controlled load lowering* means lowering a load by means of a mechanical hoist drum device that allows a hoisted load to be lowered with maximum control using the ___ or hydraulic components of the hoist mechanism.
    (a) drum brake
    (b) brake drum
    (c) gear train
    (d) gearing system
    Answer: (c) gear train § 1926.1401 Definitions Subpart CC

§1926.1401 Definitions
36. *Controlled load lowering* requires the use of the hoist ___, rather than the hoist ___, to lower the load.
    (a) drive motor, brake
    (b) brake, gear drive
    (c) gearing system, drive motor
    (d) cables, wires
    Answer: (a) drive motor, brake § 1926.1401 Definitions Subpart CC

Crane and Derrick Safety - Subpart CC

§1926.1401 Definition
37. *Controlling entity* means an employer that is a prime contractor, general contractor, construction manager or ___ which has the overall responsibility for the construction of the project - its planning, quality and completion.
    (a) governmental entity
    (b) any other legal entity
    (c) responsible entity
    (d) legally qualified professional entity
    Answer: (b) any other legal entity § 1926.1401 Definitions Subpart CC

§1926.1401 Definitions
38. A weight used to ____ the weight of equipment in providing stability for lifting loads by ____ those loads is defined by this subpart as a ___.
    (a) counterbalance, compensating for, Counterweight
    (b) compensate for, offsetting, Counterbalance weight
    (c) counter weight, offsetting, Counterbalance
    (d) supplement, counterbalancing, Counterweight
    Answer: (d) supplement, counterbalancing, Counterweight § 1926.1401 Definitions Subpart CC

§1926.1401 Definitions
39. *Crane/derrick* includes all ___ covered by this subpart.
    (a) cranes and derricks
    (b) machine equipment
    (c) power driven
    (d) equipment
    Answer: (d) equipment § 1926.1401 Definitions Subpart CC

§1926.1401 Definitions
40. *Crawler crane* means equipment that has a type of base mounting which incorporates a continuous belt of ___ driven track.
    (a) link
    (b) sprocket
    (c) bogey-wheel
    (d) flexible
    Answer: (c) sprocket § 1926.1401 Definitions Subpart CC

§1926.1401 Definitions
41. According to 29 CFR OSHA Part 1926 Definitions Subpart CC: *Crossover points* means locations on a wire rope which is ____ on a drum where one layer of rope climbs up on and crosses over the previous layer.
    (a) wound
    (b) wrapped
    (c) coiled
    (d) spooled
    Answer: (d) spooled § 1926.1401 Definitions Subpart CC

Crane and Derrick Safety - Subpart CC

§1926.1401 Definitions

42. *Crossover points* take place at each flange of the drum as the rope is spooled onto the drum, reaches the flange, and begins to ___ back in the opposite direction.
    (a) wind
    (b) wrap
    (c) coil
    (d) run
    Answer: (b) wrap § 1926.1401 Definitions Subpart CC

§1926.1401 Definitions

43. A line of communication assigned by the employer who controls the communication system to only one signal person and crane/derrick or to a coordinated group of cranes/derricks/signal person(s) is defined by this subpart as ___.
    (a) *Dedicated channel*
    (b) *Isolated channel*
    (c) *Reserved channel*
    (d) *Restricted channel*
    Answer: (a) *Dedicated channel* § 1926.1401 Definitions Subpart CC

§1926.1401 Definitions

44. A machine that is designed to function exclusively as a pile-driver is defined by this subpart as a ___. (note - there is only one correct answer - the OSHA 1926 text Subpart Answer)
    (a) Pile driver
    (b) Dedicated pile-driver
    (c) Pile Driver
    (d) Dedicated Pile-Driver
    Answer: (b) Dedicated pile-driver § 1926.1401 Definitions Subpart CC

§1926.1401 Definitions

45. *Dedicated spotter (power lines):* To be considered a dedicated spotter, the requirements of §1926.1428 (Signal persons qualifications) must be met and his/her sole responsibility is to ____ the separation between the power line and the equipment, load line, and load (including lifting and accessories), and ensure through communication with the operator that the applicable minimum approach distance is not _____.
    (a) observe, breached
    (b) verify, compromised
    (c) watch, breached
    (d) warn if, maintained
    Answer: (c) watch, breached § 1926.1401 Definitions Subpart CC

Crane and Derrick Safety - Subpart CC

§1926.1401 Definitions
46. *Directly under the load* means a part or all of an ___ is directly beneath the load.
    (a) person
    (b) individual
    (c) object
    (d) employee
    Answer: (d) employee § 1926.1401 Definitions Subpart CC

§1926.1401 Definitions
47. *Dismantling* includes partial dismantling (such as to ___ a boom or substitute a different component).
    (a) shorten
    (b) lengthen
    (c) change
    (d) modify
    Answer: (a) shorten § 1926.1401 Definitions Subpart CC

§1926.1401 Definitions
48. A device on a crane or hoist which indicates in which direction and at what relative speed a particular hoist drum is turning is defined by this subpart as a ___.
    (a) *Drum rotation indicator*
    (b) *Drum rotation counter*
    (c) *Drum speed counter*
    (d) *Drum indicator*
    Answer: (a) *Drum rotation indicator* § 1926.1401 Definitions Subpart CC

§1926.1401 Definitions
49. When a person, object, or equipment makes contact or comes in close proximity with an energized conductor or equipment that allows the passage of a current. This is defined by this subpart as ___.
    (a) *Energized*
    (b) *In contact*
    (c) *Electrical contact*
    (d) *Endangered*
    Answer: (c) *Electrical contact* § 1926.1401 Definitions Subpart CC

§1926.1401 Definitions
50. *Employer-made equipment* means ___ cranes/derricks designed and built by an employer for the employer's own use.
    (a) floating
    (b) modified
    (c) altered
    (d) specialized
    Answer: (a) floating § 1926.1401 Definitions Subpart CC

Crane and Derrick Safety - Subpart CC

§1926.1401 Definitions
51. *Encroachment* is where any part of the crane, ___, or load (including rigging and lifting accessories) ___ a minimum clearance distance that this subpart requires to be maintained from a power line.
    (a) load line, breaches
    (b) lift line, closes on
    (c) line, crosses
    (d) load, approaches
    Answer: (a) load line, breaches § 1926.1401 Definitions Subpart CC

§1926.1401 Definitions
52. *Equipment* means equipment covered by this ___.
    (a) part
    (b) subpart
    (c) section
    (d) paragraph
    Answer: (b) subpart § 1926.1401 Definitions Subpart CC

§1926.1401 Definitions
53. *Equipment criteria* means instructions, recommendations, limitations and ___.
    (a) operating instructions
    (b) operating procedures
    (c) specifications
    (d) qualifications
    Answer: (c) specifications § 1926.1401 Definitions Subpart CC

§1926.1401 Definitions
54. *Fall protection equipment* means guardrail systems, safety net systems, personal fall arrest systems, ___ or fall restraint systems.
    (a) anchoring systems
    (b) safety harness systems
    (c) positioning device systems
    (d) multi-purpose protection systems
    Answer: (c) positioning device systems § 1926.1401 Definitions Subpart CC

§1926.1401 Definitions
55. *Fall restraint* system means a fall protection system that prevents the user from falling ___.
    (a) uncontrolled
    (b) more than three feet
    (c) more than six feet
    (d) any distance
    Answer: (d) any distance § 1926.1401 Definitions Subpart CC

Crane and Derrick Safety - Subpart CC

§1926.1401 Definitions
56. The system is comprised of either a body belt or body harness, along with an anchorage, connectors, and other equipment. From _____.
    (a)　1926.1401 Definitions *Fall Protection Equipment*
    (b)　1926.1401 Definitions *Fall protection equipment*
    (c)　1926.1401Definitions *Fall Restraint System*
    (d)　1926.1401 Definitions *Fall restraint system*
    Answer: (d) 1926.1401 Definitions *Fall restraint system* § 1926.1401 Definitions Subpart CC (only answer)

§1926.1401 Definitions
57. The other components typically include a lanyard, and may also include a ___ and other devices.
    (a)　lifeline
    (b)　safety line
    (c)　harness
    (d)　belt
    Answer: (a) lifeline § 1926.1401 Definitions Subpart CC *Fall restraint system*

§1926.1401 Definitions
58. *Fall zone* means the area (including but not limited to the area ___ beneath the load) in which it is reasonably foreseeable that partially or completely suspended materials could fall in the event of an accident.
    (a)　approximately
    (b)　generally
    (c)　directly
    (d)　reasonably
    Answer: (c) directly § 1926.1401 Definitions Subpart CC

§1926.1401 Definitions
59. *Flange points* are points of ___ between rope and drum flange where the rope changes ___.
    (a)　contact, layers
    (b)　friction, direction
    (c)　contact, direction
    (d)　load, layers
    Answer: (a) contact, layers § 1926.1401 Definitions Subpart CC

§1926.1401 Definitions
60. *Floating cranes/derricks* means equipment designed by the manufacturer (or employer) for marine use by ____ attachment to a barge, pontoons, vessel or other means of flotation.
    (a)　temporary
    (b)　permanent
    (c)　welding
    (d)　bolting
    Answer: (b) permanent § 1926.1401 Definitions Subpart CC

A Ficus Tree Publishing LLC. Quick Notes Page

DU VALLS
OSHA 1926 Subpart CC — Cranes and Derricks in Construction
OSHA 1926.1401 Definitions
Instructors Manual 2014 Edition
OSHA Test CC - 3

1926.1401 Definitions

§1926.1401 Definitions
1. *For example* means ___.
   (a) "an example"
   (b) "one example"
   (c) "One example, although there are others"
   (d) "One example, although there are many others"
   Answer: (c) "One example, although there are others" § 1926.1401 Definitions Subpart CC

§1926.1401 Definitions
2. *Free fall* (of the load line) means that only the brake is used to ___ the decent of the load line (the drive mechanism is not used to drive the load down faster or retard its lowering).
   (a) control
   (b) slow
   (c) regulate
   (d) stop
   Answer: (c) regulate § 1926.1401 Definitions Subpart CC

§1926.1401 Definitions
3. *Free surface effect* is the uncontrolled ___ movements of liquids in compartments which reduce a vessel's ___ stability.
   (a) flowing, transverse
   (b) transverse, transverse
   (c) uncompressible, horizontal
   (d) incompressible, lateral
   Answer: (b) transverse, transverse § 1926.1401 Definitions Subpart CC

§1926.1401 Definitions
4. *Hoist* means a ___ device for lifting and lowering loads by winding a line onto or off a drum.
   (a) drum type mechanical
   (b) cylindrical type
   (c) power driven
   (d) mechanical
   Answer: (d) mechanical § 1926.1401 Definitions Subpart CC

Crane and Derrick Safety - Subpart CC

§1926.1401 Definitions
5. *Hoisting* is the act of raising, lowering or otherwise moving a load in the air with the equipment covered by ____.
   (a) heavy padding
   (b) nets
   (c) straps
   (d) this standard
   Answer: (d) this standard § 1926.1401 Definitions Subpart CC

§1926.1401 Definitions
6. As used in this standard, "hoisting" can be done by means other than ___ equipment.
   (a) hoisting
   (b) cranes
   (c) derricks
   (d) wire rope/hoist drum
   Answer: (d) wire rope/hoist drum § 1926.1401 Definitions Subpart CC

§1926.1401 Definitions
7. *Include/including* means "including, ___".
   (a) but not specific
   (b) but specific
   (c) but not limited to
   (d) but not limited
   Answer: (c) but not limited to § 1926.1401 Definitions Subpart CC

§1926.1401 Definitions
8. *Insulating link/device* means an insulating device listed, labeled, or accepted by a Nationally Recognized Testing laboratory in accordance with 29 CFR ___.
   (a) 1903.7
   (b) 1904.33
   (c) 1910.7
   (d) 1926.27(d)
   Answer: (c) 1910.7 § 1926.1401 Definitions Subpart CC

§1926.1401 Definitions
9. *Jib stop* (also referred to as a jib backstop), is the same type of device as a boom stop but is used for a ____.
   (a) fixed jib
   (b) fixed or lufting jib
   (c) lufting jib
   (d) swing brake
   Answer: (b) fixed or lufting jib § 1926.1401 Definitions Subpart CC

Crane and Derrick Safety - Subpart CC

§1926.1401 Definitions
10. *Land crane/derrick* is equipment not originally designed by the manufacturer for marine use by permanent attachment to barges, ___, vessels, or other means of floatation.
    (a) ships
    (b) pontoons
    (c) outriggers
    (d) sponsons
    Answer: (b) pontoons § 1926.1401 Definitions Subpart CC

§1926.1401 Definitions
11. *List* means the angle of ___ about the longitudinal axis of a barge, pontoons vessel or other means of floatation.
    (a) deflection
    (b) inclination
    (c) incident
    (d) dihedral
    Answer: (b) inclination § 1926.1401 Definitions Subpart CC

§1926.1401 Definitions
12. *Load* refers to the object(s) being hoisted and/or the weight of object(s); both uses refer to the load-attaching equipment, such as, the load ___, ropes, slings, shackles, and other ancillary attachments.
    (a) block
    (b) counter-balance
    (c) counter-weight
    (d) lines
    Answer: (a) block § 1926.1401 Definitions Subpart CC

§1926.1401 Definitions
13. *Load moment (or rated capacity) indicator* means a system which aids the equipment operator by ____ (directly or indirectly) the ____ moment of the equipment, i.e., load multiplied by radius.
    (a) warning, inertia
    (b) sensing, overturning
    (c) warning, overloading
    (d) sensing, overloading
    Answer: (b) sensing, overturning § 1926.1401 Definitions Subpart CC

§1926.1401 Definitions
14. It compares this lifting condition to the equipment's rated capacity, and when the rated capacity is reached it shuts off power to those equipment functions which can increase the ___ of loading on the equipment, e.g., hoisting, telescoping out, or lufting out.
    (a) dynamic
    (b) severity
    (c) pressure
    (d) forces
    Answer: (b) severity § 1926.1401 Definitions Subpart CC

Crane and Derrick Safety - Subpart CC

§1926.1401 Definitions

15. Typically, those functions which decrease the severity of loading on the equipment remain ____, e.g., lowering, telescoping in, or lufting in.
    (a) locked down
    (b) inoperative
    (c) operational
    (d) functional
    Answer: (c) operational § 1926.1401 Definitions Subpart CC

§1926.1401 Definitions

16. *Locomotive crane* means a crane mounted on a base or ____ equipped to travel on a railroad track.
    (a) platform
    (b) cage
    (c) reinforced car
    (d) car
    Answer: (d) car § 1926.1401 Definitions Subpart CC

§1926.1401 Definitions

17. *Luffing jib limiting device* is similar to a boom hoist limiting device, except that it ___.
    (a) limits the movement of the jib
    (b) restricts and limits the movement of the jib
    (c) limits the movement of the luffing jib
    (d) restrict and limits the movement of the luffing jib
    Answer: (c) limits the movement of the luffing jib § 1926.1401 Definitions Subpart CC

§1926.1401 Definitions

18. *Marine hoisted personnel transfer device* means a device, such as a "transfer net," that is designed to protect employees being hoisted during a marine transfer and to facilitate ___.
    (a) safe, efficient entry and exit from the device
    (b) rapid entry into and exit from the device
    (c) safe, quick and efficient entry into and exit from the personnel lift
    (d) the transfer and placement of employees for and during overwater operations
    Answer: (b) rapid entry into and exit from the device §1926.1401 Definitions Subpart CC

§1926.1401 Definitions

19. Such devices do not include ___ when hoisted by equipment covered in this standard.
    (a) personnel platforms
    (b) boatswain's chairs
    (c) chicken ladders
    (d) scaffolds
    Answer: (b) boatswain's chairs § 1926.1401 Definitions Subpart CC

Crane and Derrick Safety - Subpart CC

§1926.1401 Definitions
20. *Marine worksite* means ___.
    (a) a construction worksite located in, on or above the water
    (b) any construction worksite located in, on or above the water
    (c) any construction worksite located in, on, above or submerged in water
    (d) all construction conduced above, in, on or below the surface of water
    Answer: (a) a construction worksite located in, on or above the water § 1926.1401 Definitions Subpart CC

§1926.1401 Definitions
21. *Mobil crane* means a lifting device incorporating a cable suspended ___ boom or hydraulic telescopic boom designed to be moved between operating locations by transport over the road.
    (a) steel
    (b) lattice
    (c) rigid
    (d) reinforced
    Answer: (b) lattice § 1926.1401 Definitions Subpart CC

§1926.1401 Definitions
22. *Moving point-to-point* means the times during which an employee is in the process of going to or coming from a ___.
    (a) job
    (b) project
    (c) jobsite
    (d) work station
    Answer: (d) work station § 1926.1401 Definitions Subpart CC

§1926.1401 Definitions
23. *Multi-purpose machine* means machine that is designed to be ___ in various ways, at least one of which allows it to hoist (by means of a winch or hook) and horizontally move a suspended load.
    (a) changed
    (b) modified
    (c) configured
    (d) altered
    Answer: (c) configured § 1926.1401 Definitions Subpart CC

§1926.1401 Definitions
24. For example, a machine that can rotate and be configured with removable forks/tongs (for use as a forklift) or with a winch pack, jib (with a hook at the end) or a jib used in conjunction with a ___.
    (a) wrench
    (b) come-a-long
    (c) winch
    (d) telescoping boom
    Answer: (c) winch § 1926.1401 Definitions Subpart CC

Crane and Derrick Safety - Subpart CC

§1926.1401 Definitions
25. When configured with the forks/tongs, it is ___ by this subpart.
    (a) not covered
    (b) not included
    (c) covered
    (d) included
    Answer: (a) not covered § 1926.1401 Definitions Subpart CC

§1926.1401 Definitions
26. When configured with a winch pack, jib (with a hook at the end) or jib used in conjunction with a winch, it ___.
    (a) is also, not covered by this subpart
    (b) is covered by this subpart
    (c) is exempted from this subpart
    (d) is not exempted from this subpart
    Answer: (b) is covered by this subpart § 1926.1401 Definitions Subpart CC

§1926.1401 Definitions
27. *Nationally recognized accrediting agency* is an organization that, due to its ___ and ___, is widely recognized as competent to accredit testing organizations.
    (a) reputation, expertise
    (b) expertise, proven experience
    (c) independence, expertise
    (d) experience, independence
    Answer: (c) independence, expertise § 1926.1401 Definitions Subpart CC

§1926.1401 Definitions
28. Examples of such accrediting agencies include, but are not limited to, the National Commission for Certifying Agencies and the ___.
    (a) National Scientific Laboratories
    (b) NOAA
    (c) American National Standards Institute
    (d) Concrete Reinforcing Steel Institute
    Answer: (c) American National Standards Institute (only correct answer) §1926.1401 Definitions Subpart CC

§1926.1401 Definitions
29. *Nonconductive* means that, because of the nature and condition of the materials used, and the conditions of use (including environmental conditions and condition of material), the object in question has the property of not ___ (that is, it has high dielectric properties offering a high resistance to the passage of current under the conditions of use).
    (a) being conductive
    (b) becoming energized
    (c) carrying an electrical charge
    (d) being capable of carrying an electrical current
    Answer: (b) becoming energized § 1926.1401 Definitions Subpart CC

Crane and Derrick Safety - Subpart CC

§1926.1401 Definitions
30. *Operational aids* are devices that assist the operator in the safe operation of the crane by providing ___ or automatically taking control of a crane function.
   (a) information
   (b) power boosting
   (c) control over-rides
   (d) kill switches
   Answer: (a) information § 1926.1401 Definitions Subpart CC

§1926.1401 Definitions
31. *Operational aids* include, but are not limited to, the devices listed in § 1926.____ ("listed operational aids").
   (a) 1400
   (b) 1403
   (c) 1416
   (d) 1492
   Answer: (c) 1416 § 1926.1401 Definitions Subpart CC

§1926.1401 Definitions
32. *Operational controls* means, ___, ___, ___, and other devices for controlling equipment operation.
   (a) levers, switches, pedals
   (b) switches, levers, pedals
   (c) pedals, levers, switches
   (d) pedals, switches, levers
   Answer: (a) levers, switches, pedals (only correct answer) § 1926.1401 Definitions Subpart CC

§1926.1401 Definitions
33. *Operator* means ____.
   (a) he or she who operates the equipment
   (b) he or she who is qualified to operate the equipment
   (c) he or she who is operating the equipment
   (d) a person who is operating the equipment
   Answer: (d) a person who is operating the equipment § 1926.1401 Definitions Subpart CC

§1926.1401 Definitions
34. *Overhead and gantry cranes* includes overhead/bridge cranes, semigantry, ___ gantry, wall cranes, storage bridge cranes, launching cranes, and similar equipment irrespective of whether it travels on tracks, wheels, or other means.
   (a) lattice
   (b) fixed
   (c) cantilevered
   (d) inverted beam
   Answer: (c) cantilevered § 1926.1401 Definitions Subpart CC

Crane and Derrick Safety - Subpart CC

§1926.1401 Definitions
35. *Paragraph* refers to a paragraph in the same section of this subpart that the word "paragraph" is used, unless ____.
    (a) specified elsewhere
    (b) specified to another subpart
    (c) specified to another part
    (d) otherwise specified
    Answer: (d) otherwise specified § 1926.1401 Definitions Subpart CC

§1926.1401 Definitions
36. *Pendants* includes both ___ and ___ types:
    (a) cable, solid
    (b) wire, bar
    (c) bar, wire
    (d) steel, natural rope
    Answer: (b) wire, bar § 1926.1401 Definitions Subpart CC

§1926.1401 Definitions
37. *Pendants - Wire Type*: a fixed length of wire rope with mechanical fittings at both ends for pinning ____ of wire rope together.
    (a) strands
    (b) lengths
    (c) sections
    (d) segments
    Answer: (d) segments § 1926.1401 Definitions Subpart CC

§1926.1401 Definitions
38. *Pendants - Bar Type*: Instead of rope, a bar is used. Pendants are typically used in a lattice boom system to easily change the length of the boom ___ without completely changing the ___ when the boom length is increased or decreased.
    (a) suspension, system
    (b) suspension system, rope on the drum
    (c) cantilever, suspension system
    (d) rope on the drum, suspension
    Answer: (b) suspension system, rope on the drum § 1926.1401 Definitions Subpart CC

§1926.1401 Definitions
39. *Personal fall arrest system* means a system used to arrest an employee in a fall from a ____.
    (a) elevated walking/working surface
    (b) Hammerhead crane boom
    (c) derrick bridge
    (d) working level
    Answer: (d) working level § 1926.1401 Definitions Subpart CC

Crane and Derrick Safety - Subpart CC

§1926.1401 Definitions
40. *A personal fall arrest system* consists of an anchorage, connectors, body harness and may include a lanyard ___, lifeline, or suitable combination of these.
    (a) safety belt
    (b) body harness and safety belt
    (c) deceleration device
    (d) shock cord
    Answer: (c) deceleration device § 1926.1401 Definitions Subpart CC

§1926.1401 Definitions
41. *Portal crane* is a type of crane consisting of a ____ upperstructure, hoist machinery, and boom mounted on top of a structural gantry which may be fixed in one location or have travel capability.
    (a) rotating
    (b) revolving
    (c) stationary
    (d) tracked
    Answer: (a) rotating § 1926.1401 Definitions Subpart CC

§1926.1401 Definitions
42. *The gantry legs or columns* usually have ___ in between to allow passage of traffic beneath the gantry.
    (a) portals
    (b) portal openings
    (c) passageways
    (d) companionways
    Answer: (b) portal openings § 1926.1401 Definitions Subpart CC

§1926.1401 Definitions
43. *Power lines* mean ___.
    (a) energized lines
    (b) electric transmission lines
    (c) electric transmission and distribution lines
    (d) high voltage electric transmission and distribution lines
    Answer: (c) electric transmission and distribution lines

§1926.1401 Definitions
44. *Procedures* include, but are not limited to: Instructions, diagrams, recommendations, warnings, specifications, ___ and limitations
    (a) protocols
    (b) procedures
    (c) principles
    (d) regulations
    Answer: (a) protocols § 1926.1401 Definitions Subpart CC

Crane and Derrick Safety - Subpart CC

§1926.1401 Definitions
45. *Proximity alarm* is a device that provides a warning of ___ and that has been listed, labeled or accepted by a Nationally Recognized Testing Laboratory in accordance with 29 CFR ___.
    (a) proximity to a live power line, 1904.04
    (b) proximity to contact danger, 1910.02
    (c) proximity to a power line, 1910.7
    (d) imminent contact with an energized source, 1926.503
    Answer: (c) proximity to a power line, 1910.7 § 1926.1401 Definitions Subpart CC

§1926.1401 Definitions
46. *Qualified evaluator* (not a third party) means a person employed by the signal person's employer who has ___ that he/she is competent in accurately assessing whether individuals meet the Qualification Requirements in this subpart for a signal person.
    (a) proven
    (b) demonstrated
    (c) established
    (d) documentation
    Answer: (b) demonstrated § 1926.1401 Definitions Subpart CC

§1926.1401 Definitions
47. *Qualified evaluator* (third party) means an entity that, due to its independence and expertise, has ___ that it is competent in accurately accessing whether individuals meet the Qualification Requirements in this subpart for a signal person.
    (a) established
    (b) demonstrated
    (c) proven
    (d) documented proof
    Answer: (b) demonstrated § 1926.1401 Definitions Subpart CC

§1926.1401 Definitions
48. *Qualified person* means a person who, by possession of a recognized degree, certificate, or professional standing, or who by extensive knowledge, training and experience, ___ demonstrated the ability to solve/resolve problems relating to the subject matter, the work, or the project.
    (a) has
    (b) did
    (c) successfully
    (d) substantially
    Answer: (c) successfully § 1926.1401 Definitions Subpart CC

Crane and Derrick Safety - Subpart CC

§1926.1401 Definitions
49. *Qualified rigger* is a rigger who meets the criteria for a ___.
    (a) Qualified person
    (b) Qualified evaluator
    (c) Competent Person
    (d) Competent person
    Answer: (a) Qualified person § 1926.1401 Definitions Subpart CC

§1926.1401 Definitions
50. *Range control limit device* is a device that can be set by an equipment operator to limit movement of the boom or jib tip to a ___ or multiple ___.
    (a) specific setting, settings
    (b) specific angle, angles
    (c) set degree, degrees
    (d) plane, planes
    Answer: (d) plane, planes § 1926.1401 Definitions Subpart CC

§1926.1401 Definitions
51. *Range control warning device* is a device that can be set by an equipment operator to warn that the boom or jib tip is at a ___ or multiple ___.
    (a) plane, planes
    (b) set degree, degrees
    (c) specific angle, angles
    (d) specific setting, settings
    Answer: (a) plane, planes § 1926.1401 Definitions Subpart CC

§1926.1401 Definitions
52. *Rated capacity* means the maximum working load permitted by the manufacturer under ____ working conditions.
    (a) specific
    (b) specified
    (c) stated
    (d) standard
    Answer: (b) specified § 1926.1401 Definitions Subpart CC

§1926.1401 Definitions
53. Such working conditions typically include a specific combination of factors such as equipment configuration, ___, boom length, and other parameters of use.
    (a) radii
    (b) radius
    (c) swing arc
    (d) reach
    Answer: (a) radii § 1926.1401 Definitions Subpart CC

For *Rated capacity indicator*: See load moment indicator. For *Rated capacity limiter*: See load moment limiter.

Crane and Derrick Safety - Subpart CC

§1926.1401 Definitions

54. *Repetitive pickup points* refer to, when operating a ___ operation, the rope being used on a single layer and being spooled repetitively over a short portion of the drum.
    (a) closed cycle
    (b) repeat cycle
    (c) short cycle
    (d) fast cycle
    Answer: (c) short cycle § 1926.1401 Definitions Subpart CC

§1926.1401 Definitions

55. *Running wire rope* means a wire rope that moves over ____ or ____.
    (a) block, tackle
    (b) pulleys, drums
    (c) rollers, pulleys
    (d) sheaves, drums
    Answer: (d) sheaves, drums § 1926.1401 Definitions Subpart CC

§1926.1401 Definitions

56. *Runway* means a ____, level surface designed, prepared and designated as a path of travel for the weight and configuration of the crane being used to lift and travel with the crane suspended platform. An existing surface may be used as long as it meets these criteria.
    (a) solid
    (b) compacted
    (c) firm
    (d) paved
    Answer: firm § 1926.1401 Definitions Subpart CC

§1926.1401 Definitions

57. *Section* means a section of this subpart, unless ___.
    (a) otherwise noted
    (b) stated otherwise
    (c) noted
    (d) otherwise specified
    Answer: (d) otherwise specified § 1926.1401 Definitions Subpart CC

§1926.1401 Definitions

58. *Sideboom crane* means a track-type or wheel-type tractor having a boom mounted on the side of the tractor, used for lifting, lowering or transporting a load suspended on the ___.
    (a) boom
    (b) hook
    (c) boom hook
    (d) load hook
    Answer: (d) load hook § 1926.1401 Definitions Subpart CC

Crane and Derrick Safety - Subpart CC

§1926.1401 Definitions
59. The boom or load can be lifted or lowered in a ___ only.
    (a) vertical direction
    (b) rotating movement
    (c) stationary position
    (d) transverse movement
    Answer: (a) vertical direction § 1926.1401 Definitions Subpart CC

§1926.1401 Definitions
60. *Special hazard warning* means warning of ___ hazards (for example, proximity of power lines).
    (a) specific
    (b) unexpected
    (c) site-specific
    (d) common-site
    Answer: (c) site-specific § 1926.1401 Definitions Subpart CC

A Ficus Tree Publishing LLC. Quick Notes Page

DU VALLS
OSHA 1926 Subpart CC — Cranes and Derricks in Construction
OSHA 1926.1401 Definitions
Instructors Manual 2014 Edition
OSHA Test CC - 4

1926.1401 Definitions

§1926.1401 Definitions

1. *Stability (floatation device)* means the tendency of a barge, pontoons, vessel or other means of flotation to return to an ___ after having been inclined by an external force.
   - (a) equilibrium point
   - (b) upright point
   - (c) level position
   - (d) upright position

   Answer: (d) upright position § 1926.1401 Definitions Subpart CC

§1926.1401 Definitions

2. *Standard Method* means the protocol in Appendix A of this subpart for ___.
   - (a) procedures
   - (b) instructions
   - (c) hand signals
   - (d) definitions

   Answer: (c) hand signals § 1926.1401 Definitions Subpart CC

§1926.1401 Definitions

3. *Such as* means "___".
   - (a) not specific
   - (b) similar to
   - (c) such as, but not limited to
   - (d) comparable to

   Answer: (c) such as, but not limited to § 1926.1401 Definitions Subpart CC

§1926.1401 Definitions

4. *Superstructure*: See ___
   - (a) Elevated structures
   - (b) Overhead
   - (c) Hammerhead cranes
   - (d) Upperworks

   Answer: (d) Upperworks § 1926.1401 Definitions Subpart CC

Crane and Derrick Safety - Subpart CC

§1926.1401 Definitions
5. *Tagline* means a rope (usually fiber) attached to a lifted load for purposes of controlling ___ and ___ motions or used to stabilize a bucket or magnet during material handling operations.
   (a) swinging, swaying
   (b) rotation, spinning
   (c) pendulum motion, rotation
   (d) load spinning, pendular motion
   Answer: (d) load spinning, pendular motion § 1926.1401 Definitions Subpart CC

§1926.1401 Definitions
6. *Tender* means an individual responsible for monitoring and communicating with a ____.
   (a) operator
   (b) signal person
   (c) diver
   (d) equipment operator
   Answer: (c) diver § 1926.1401 Definitions Subpart CC

§1926.1401 Definitions
7. *Tilt up or tilt down operation* down means raising or lowering a load from the ___ to ___ or ___ to ___.
   (a) horizontal, vertical, vertical, horizontal
   (b) level, vertical, vertical, level
   (c) ground, another level, another level, ground
   (d) horizontal, inclined, inclined, horizontal
   Answer: (a) horizontal, vertical, vertical, horizontal § 1926.1401 Definitions Subpart CC

§1926.1401 Definitions
8. Tower crane is a type of lifting structure which utilizes a vertical ____ or tower to support a working boom (jib) in an elevated position.
   (a) structure
   (b) foundation
   (c) lift
   (d) mast
   Answer: (d) mast § 1926.1401 Definitions Subpart CC

§1926.1401 Definitions
9. Loads are suspended from the ___.
   (a) boom
   (b) jib
   (c) hook
   (d) working boom
   Answer: (d) working boom § 1926.1401 Definitions (second sentence) Subpart CC

Crane and Derrick Safety - Subpart CC

§1926.1401 Definitions
10. While the working boom may be of the fixed type (horizontal or angled) or have luffing capability, it can always rotate to swing loads, either by rotating on the on the top of the tower (____) or by the rotation of the tower (____).
    (a) top slewing, bottom slewing
    (b) top swinging, bottom swinging
    (c) top rotation, bottom rotation
    (d) vertical swing out, vertical swing in
    Answer: (a) top slewing, bottom slewing § 1926.1401 Definitions Subpart CC

§1926.1401 Definitions
11. The tower base may be fixed in one location or ___ and movable between locations.
    (a) tracked
    (b) ballasted
    (c) rail mounted
    (d) barge mounted
    Answer: (b) ballasted § 1926.1401 Definitions Subpart CC

§1926.1401 Definitions
12. Mobile cranes that are configured with ___ jib and/or tower attachments are not considered tower cranes under this section.
    (a) luffing
    (b) inclined
    (c) sloping
    (d) angled
    Answer: (a) luffing § 1926.1401 Definitions Subpart CC

§1926.1401 Definitions
13. *Travel bogie (tower cranes)* is an assembly of two or more axels arranged to permit ___ and equalize the loading on the wheels.
    (a) transit
    (b) vehicle wheel displacement
    (c) tower crane wheel balancing
    (d) tower crane wheel alignment
    Answer: (b) vehicle wheel displacement § 1926.1401 Definitions Subpart CC

§1926.1401 Definitions
14. *Trim* means angle of ___ about the transverse axis of a barge, pontoons, vessel or other means of flotation.
    (a) inclination
    (b) repose
    (c) rise
    (d) the boom
    Answer: (a) inclination § 1926.1401 Definitions Subpart CC

Crane and Derrick Safety - Subpart CC

§1926.1401 Definitions
15. *Two blocking* means a condition in which a component that is uppermost on the hoist line such as a load block, hook block, overhaul ball, or similar component, comes in contact with the boom tip, ___ or similar component. This binds the system and continued application of power can cause failure of the hoist ____ or other component.
    (a) fixed upper block, rope
    (b) fixed secondary block, wire
    (c) mobile upper block, cable
    (d) sliding upper block, rope
    Answer: (a) fixed upper block, rope § 1926.1401 Definitions Subpart CC

§1926.1401 Definitions
16. *Unavailable Procedures* means ___.
    (a) procedures unavailable from the manufacturer
    (b) procedures that are no longer available from the manufacturer
    (c) procedures that are no longer available from the manufacturer, or have never been available, from the manufacturer
    (d) any out of date procedure or set of instructions that have never been available
    Answer: (c) procedures that are no longer available from the manufacturer, or have never been available from the manufacturer § 1926.1401 Definitions Subpart CC

§1926.1401 Definitions
17. *Upperworks* means the revolving frame of equipment on which the operating machinery (and in many cases the engine) are mounted along with the operator's ____.
    (a) control pedals
    (b) control levers
    (c) engine operating controls
    (d) cab
    Answer: (d) cab § 1926.1401 Definitions Subpart CC

§1926.1401 Definitions
18. The counterweight is typically supported on the rear of the upperstructure and the boom or other front end attachment is mounted ___.
    (a) backward
    (b) frontward
    (c) on front end tracks
    (d) on the front
    Answer: (d) on the front § 1926.1401 Definitions Subpart CC

§1926.1401 Definitions
19. *Up to* means "___"
    (a) Up to a specific point
    (b) Up to a specific point on the crane or boom
    (c) to the uppermost transverse running and standing ropes
    (d) up to and including
    Answer: (d) up to and including § 1926.1401 Definitions Subpart CC

Crane and Derrick Safety - Subpart CC

§1926.1401 Definitions

20. Wire rope means a flexible rope constructed by laying steel wires into various patterns of multi-wired strands a core system to produce a ___ rope.
    (a) symmetrical wound
    (b) asymmetrical wound
    (c) helically wound
    (d) hemispheric ally wound

    Answer: (c) helically wound § 1926.1401 Definitions Subpart CC

A Ficus Tree Publishing LLC. Quick Notes Page

DU VALLS
OSHA 1926 Subpart CC — Cranes and Derricks in Construction
OSHA 1926.1402 Ground Conditions
Instructors Manual 2014 Edition
OSHA Test CC - 5

§1926.1402 Ground Conditions - Definitions
1. 29CFR OSHA Part 1926 Safety and Health Regulations in Construction Subpart CC Cranes & Derricks in Construction, Standard number 1402 Ground Conditions, 1926.1402(a) discusses___.
   - (a) Cranes
   - (b) Derricks
   - (c) Ground Conditions
   - (d) Definitions

   Answer: (d) Definitions § 1926.1402(a) Ground Conditions, Subpart CC

§1926.1402 (a)(1) Ground Conditions
2. 1926.1402(a)(1) discusses ___.
   - (a) Cranes
   - (b) Derricks
   - (c) Ground conditions
   - (d) Definitions

   Answer: (c) Ground conditions § 1926.1402(a)(1) Ground conditions Subpart CC

§1926.1402 (a)(1) Ground Conditions
3. "*Ground conditions*" means the ability of the ground to support equipment (including slope, compaction, and _____).
   - (a) moisture content
   - (b) soil structure
   - (c) firmness
   - (d) soil composition

   Answer: (c) firmness § 1926.1402(a)(1) Ground conditions Subpart CC

§1926.1402 (a)(2) Ground Conditions
4. "Supporting materials" means blocking, mats, cribbing, ____ (in marshes/wetlands), or similar supporting materials or devices.
   - (a) waders
   - (b) boats
   - (c) marsh buggies
   - (d) swamp tractors

   Answer: (c) marsh buggies §1926.1402(a)(2) Ground conditions Subpart CC

Crane and Derrick Safety - Subpart CC

§1926.1402 (b) Ground Conditions

5. The equipment must not be assembled or used unless ground conditions are firm, drained, and ____ to a sufficient so that, in conjunction (if necessary) with the use of supporting materials, the equipment manufacturer's specifications for adequate support and degree of level of the equipment are met. The requirement for the ground to be drained does not apply to wetlands.
   (a) leveled
   (b) cleared
   (c) graded
   (d) compacted
   Answer: (c) graded §1926.1402(b) Ground conditions Subpart CC

§1926.1402 (c) Ground Conditions

6. 1926.1402(c) states ____.
   (a) The controlling entity must:
   (b) The Prime contractor must:
   (c) The General contractor shall:
   (d) The qualifying officer shall:
   Answer: (a) The controlling entity must: § 1926.1402(c) Ground conditions Subpart CC

§1926.1402 (c)(1) Ground Conditions

7. The controlling entity must: Ensure that ground ___ necessary to meet the requirements of paragraph (___) of this section are provided.
   (a) conditions, a
   (b) preparations, b
   (c) stability, c
   (d) compaction, d
   Answer: (b) preparations, b § 1926.1402(c) and § 1926.1402(c)(1) Ground conditions Subpart CC

§1926.1402 (c)(2) Ground Conditions

8. The controlling entity must: Inform the user of the equipment and the operator of the location of ___ beneath the equipment set-up area (such as voids, tanks, utilities) if those hazards are identified in documents (such as site drawings, as-built drawings, and soil analysis) that are in the possession of the controlling entity (whether at the site or off-site) or the hazards are otherwise known to that controlling entity.
   (a) chemicals
   (b) hazards
   (c) potential problems
   (d) suspected problems
   Answer: (b) hazards § 1926,1402(c)(2) Ground conditions Subpart CC

Crane and Derrick Safety - Subpart CC

§1926.1402 (d) Ground Conditions

9. If there is no controlling entity for the project, the requirement of paragraph ___ of this section must be met by the employer that has authority at the site to make or arrange for ground preparations needed to meet paragraph (b) of this section.
   (a) (a)(1)
   (b) (b)(1)
   (c) (c)(1)
   (d) (d)(1)
   Answer: (c) (c)(1) § 1926.1402(d) Ground conditions Subpart CC

1926.1402 (e) Ground Conditions Subpart CC

10. If the A/D director or the operator determines that ground conditions do not meet the requirements in paragraph (b) of this section, that person's employer must have a discussion with the controlling entity regarding the ground ___ that are needed so that, with the use of suitable supporting materials/devices (if necessary), the requirements in paragraph (b) of this section can be met.
    (a) loading
    (b) preparations
    (c) stability
    (d) density
    Answer: (b) preparations § 1926.1402(e) Ground conditions Subpart CC

§1926.1402 (f) Ground Conditions

11. This section does not apply to cranes designed for use on railroad tracks when used on railroad tracks that are a part of the general railroad system of transportation that is regulated pursuant to the Federal Railroad Administration under 49 CFR Part ___ and that comply with applicable Federal Railroad Administration requirements.
    (a) 123
    (b) 321
    (c) 213
    (d) 312
    Answer: (c) 213 § 1926.1402(f) Ground conditions Subpart CC

A Ficus Tree Publishing LLC. Quick Notes Page

DU VALLS
OSHA 1926 Subpart CC — Cranes and Derricks in Construction
OSHA 1926.1403 Assembly/Disassembly—selection of manufacturer or employer procedures.
Instructors Manual 2014 Edition
OSHA Test CC - 6

§1926.1403 Assembly/Disassembly
1. When assembling or disassembling equipment (or attachments) the employer must comply with all applicable ___ prohibitions and must comply with either:
    (a) OSHA
    (b) OSHA regulations and
    (c) 29 CFR Part 1926 regulations and
    (d) manufacturer
    Answer: (d) manufacturer §1926.1403 Assembly/Disassembly- selection of manufacturer or employer procedures. Subpart CC

§1926.1403 Assembly/Disassembly
2. 1926.1403(a) states ___.
    (a) Employer procedures for assembly/disassembly of equipment
    (b) Employer procedures for assembly/disassembly of crane lattice boom units
    (c) Manufacturer procedures applicable to assembly/disassembly
    (d) Manufacturer procedures applicable to assembly/disassembly, or
    Answer: (d) Manufacturer procedures applicable to assembly/disassembly, or §1926.1403(a) Assembly/Disassembly - selection of manufacturer or employer procedures. Subpart CC

§1926.1403 Assembly/Disassembly
3. 1926.1403(b) states ___.
    (a) Employer procedures for assembly and disassembly
    (b) Supplemental employer procedures for assembly and disassembly
    (c) Amendments to employer procedures for assembly and disassembly
    (d) Additional amendments to employer procedures for assembly and disassembly
    Answer: (a) Employer procedures for assembly and disassembly §1926.1403 (b) Assembly/Disassembly - selection of manufacturer or employer procedures. Subpart CC

§1926.1403 Assembly/Disassembly
4. Employer procedures may be used only where the employer can demonstrate that the procedures used meet the requirements in §1926.___.
    (a) 1403
    (b) 1405
    (c) 1406
    (d) 1409
    Answer: (c) 1406 § 1926.1403(b) Assembly/Disassembly - selection of manufacturer or employer procedures. Subpart CC

Subpart CC

§1926.1403 Assembly/Disassembly

5. **Note:** The employer ___ follow manufacturer procedures when an employer uses synthetic slings during the assembly or disassembly rigging. (See § 1926.1404(r).)
    (a) shall
    (b) must
    (c) should
    (d) will

   Answer: (b) must § 1926.1403(b) Assembly/Disassembly - selection of manufacturer or employer procedures. Subpart CC

DU VALLS
OSHA 1926 Subpart CC — Cranes and Derricks in Construction
OSHA 1926.1404 Assembly/Disassembly—general requirements (applies to all assembly and disassembly operations).
Instructors Manual 2014 Edition
OSHA Test CC - 7

§1926.1404 Assembly/Disassembly-general requirements
1. 1926.1404 discusses ___.
   (a) Cranes & Derricks in Construction
   (b) Safety and Health Regulations for Construction
   (c) Assembly/Disassembly-general requirements (applies to all assembly and disassembly operations).
   (d) *Supervision-competent-qualified person*

   Answer: (c) Assembly/Disassembly-general requirements (applies to all assembly and disassembly operations). § 1926.1404 Title and Scope statement Subpart CC

§1926.1404(a) Assembly/Disassembly-general requirements
2. 1926.1404(a) discusses ___.
   (a) *Supervision*
   (b) *Supervision-competent person*
   (c) *Supervision-competent-qualified person*
   (d) *Supervision-qualified-competent person*

   Answer: (c) *Supervision-competent-qualified person* § 1926.1404(a) Assembly/Disassembly- general requirements (applies to all assembly and disassembly operations) Subpart CC

§1926.1404 (a)(1) Assembly/Disassembly-general requirements
3. Assembly/disassembly must be directed by a person who meets the criteria for both a ____ and a ____, or by a competent person who is assisted by one or more ___ ("A/D director").
   (a) rigger, operator, riggers
   (b) qualified rigger, operator, riggers
   (c) competent person, qualified rigger, qualified persons
   (d) competent person, qualified person, qualified persons

   Answer: (d) competent person, qualified person, qualified persons § 1926.1404(a)(1) Assembly/Disassembly general requirements (applies to all assembly and disassembly operations). Subpart CC

Crane and Derrick Safety - Subpart CC

§1926.1404 (a)(2) Assembly/Disassembly-general requirements

4. Where the assembly/disassembly is being performed by only one person, that person must meet the criteria for both a competent person and a qualified person. For purposes of this standard, that person is consider the ___.
   (a) Supervisor
   (b) A/D director
   (c) A/B rigger
   (d) A/C rigger

   Answer: (b) A/D director § 1926.1404(a)(2) Assembly?Disassembly7pgeneral requirements (applies to all assembly and disassembly operations). Subpart CC

§1926.1404 (b) Assembly/Disassembly-general requirements

5. *Knowledge of procedures.* The ___ must understand the applicable assembly/disassembly procedures.
   (a) A/D director
   (b) operator
   (c) rigger
   (d) employer

   Answer: (a) A/D director § 1926.1404(b) Assembly/Disassembly-general requirements (applies to all assembly and disassembly operations). Subpart CC

§1926.1404 (c)Assembly/Disassembly-general requirements

6. *Review of procedures.* The A/D director must review the applicable assembly/disassembly procedures ___ to the commencement of assembly/disassembly unless the A/D director understands the procedures and has applied them to the same type and configuration of equipment (including accessories, if any).
   (a) controls
   (b) immediately prior
   (c) immediately after
   (d) following

   Answer: (b) immediately prior § 1926.1404(c) Assembly/Disassembly-general requirements (applies to all assembly and disassembly operations). Subpart CC

§1926.1404 (d) Assembly/Disassembly-general requirements

7. 1926.1404(d) discusses ___.
   (a) *Crew instructions*
   (b) *Crew procedures*
   (c) *Crew qualifications*
   (d) *Specific crew duties*

   Answer: (a) *Crew instructions* § 1926.1404(d) Assembly/Disassembly-general requirements (applies to all assembly and disassembly operations). Subpart CC

Crane and Derrick Safety - Subpart CC

§1926.1404 Assembly/Disassembly-general requirements
8. Before commencing assembly/disassembly operations, the A/D director must ___ the crew members understand all of the following:
   (a) verify
   (b) establish
   (c) ascertain
   (d) ensure
   Answer: (d) ensure § 1926.1404(d)(1) Assembly/Disassembly-general requirements (applies to all assembly and disassembly operations). Subpart CC

§1926.1404 (d)(1)(i) Assembly/Disassembly-general requirements
9. Before commencing assembly/disassembly operations, the A/D director must ensure the crew members understand all of the following: Their tasks. ___. The hazardous positions/locations that they need to avoid.
   (a) The danger present
   (b) The hazards that are present
   (c) The hazards associated with their tasks
   (d) The dangers/hazards and risks associated with their tasks
   Answer: (c) The hazards associated with their tasks §1926.1404(d)(1) (i) Assembly/Disassembly-general requirements(applies to all assembly and disassembly operations). Subpart CC

§1926.1404 (d)(1)(Assembly/Disassembly-general requirements
10. During assembly/disassembly operations, before a crew member takes on a different task, or when adding new personnel during the operations, the requirements of paragraphs ___ through ___ of the section must be met.
    (a) (d)(1)(i), (d)(1)(ii)
    (b) (d)(1)(i), (d)(1)(iii)
    (c) (d)(1)(i), (d)(1)(iv)
    (d) (d)(1)(i), (e)(2)
    Answer: (b) (d)(1)(i) (d)(1)(iii). §1926.1404(d)(2) Assembly/Disassembly-general requirements (applies to all assembly and disassembly operations). Subpart CC

§1926.1404 (e)(1)(Assembly/Disassembly-general requirements
11. 1926.1404(e) discusses ___.
    (a) Protecting assembly/disassembly crew members
    (b) Protecting assembly/disassembly crew members during operations
    (c) Protecting assembly/disassembly crew members out of operator view
    (d) Protecting assembly/disassembly crew members out of operator view during operations
    Answer: (c) Protecting assembly/disassembly crew members out of operators view §1926.1404(e) Assembly/Disassembly-general requirements (applies to all assembly and disassembly operations). Subpart CC

Crane and Derrick Safety - Subpart CC

§1926.1404 (e)(1)(Assembly/Disassembly-general requirements

12. Before a crew member goes to a location that is out of view of the operator and is either in, on or under the equipment, or near the equipment (or load) where the crew member could be injured by movement of the equipment) or load), the crew member must ___.
    (a) inform the operator that he/she is going to that location
    (b) inform the crew chief and the operator that he/she is going to that location
    (c) request and confirm the operator has set the necessary safety locks to prevent movement
    (d) inform the operator and personally verify the proper lockout/tagout procedures are set

    Answer: (a) inform the operator that he/she is going to that location § 1926.1404(e)(1) Assembly/Disassembly-general requirements (applies to all assembly and disassembly operations). Subpart CC

§1926.1404 (e)(1)(Assembly/Disassembly-general requirements

13. Where the operator knows that a crew member went to a location covered by paragraph ___ of this section, the operator must not move any part of the equipment (or load) until the operator is informed in accordance with a prearranged system of communication that the crew member is in a safe position.
    (a) (d)(1)(ii)
    (b) (e)(1)
    (c) (g)(1)
    (d) (f)(2)(ii)

    Answer: (b) (e)(1). §1926.1404(e)(2) Assembly/Disassembly-general requirements (applies to all assembly and disassembly operations). Subpart CC

§1926.1404 (f)(Assembly/Disassembly-general requirements

14. 1926.1404(f) addresses ___.
    (a) *Working under the boom, jib or other components*
    (b) *Working under the equipment*
    (c) *Working, servicing equipment*
    (d) *Refueling operations*

    Answer: (a) Working under the boom, jib or other components. §1926.1404 (f) Assembly/Disassembly-general requirements (applies to all assembly and disassembly operations). Subpart CC

§1926.1404 (f)(1)(Assembly/Disassembly-general requirements

15. When pins (or similar devices) are being removed, employees must not be under the boom, jib, or other components, except where the requirements of paragraph ___ of this section are met.
    (a) (e)(2)
    (b) (f)(2)
    (c) (g)(2)
    (d) (h)(2)

    Answer: (b) (f)(2). §1926.1404(f)(1) Assembly/Disassembly-general requirements (applies to all assembly and disassembly operations). Subpart CC

Crane and Derrick Safety - Subpart CC

§1926.1404 (f)(2) Assembly/Disassembly-general requirements

16. *Exception.* Where the employer demonstrates that site constraints require one or more employees under the boom, jib, or other components when pins (or similar devices) are being removed, the A/D director must implement procedures that minimize the risk of unintended ___ and minimize the duration and extent of exposure under the boom. (See non-mandatory Appendix B of this subpart for an example).
    (a) rotation of the boom
    (b) collapse of the boom
    (c) failure of the boom
    (d) dangerous movement
    Answer: (d) dangerous movement. §1926.1404(f)(2) Exception. Assembly/Disassembly-general requirements (applies to all assembly and disassembly operations). Subpart CC

§1926.1404 (g) Assembly/Disassembly-general requirements

17. *Capacity limits.* During all phases of assembly/disassembly, rated capacity limits for loads imposed on the equipment, equipment components (including rigging), ___, and equipment accessories, must not be exceeded for the equipment being assembled/disassembled.
    (a) hooks
    (b) lifting hooks
    (c) lifting lugs
    (d) shackles
    Answer: (c) lifting lugs § 1926.1404 (g) Assembly/Disassembly-general requirements (applies to all assembly and disassembly operations). Subpart CC

§1926.1404 (h) Assembly/Disassembly-general requirements

18. 1926.1404(h) addresses ___.
    (a) Hazards
    (b) Specific hazards
    (c) Addressing specific hazards
    (d) Addressing specific hazards regarding assembly/disassembly
    Answer: (c) Addressing specific hazards § 1926.1404(h) Assembly/Disassembly-general requirements (applies to all assembly and disassembly operations) Subpart CC

§1926.1404 (h) Assembly/Disassembly-general requirements

19. *Addressing specific hazards.* The A/D director supervising the assembly/disassembly operation must address the hazards ___, which include:
    (a) of assembly/disassembly
    (b) associated with the work
    (c) associated with crane and derrick assembly and disassembly
    (d) associated with the operation
    Answer: (d) associated with the operation §1926.1404(h) Assembly/Disassembly-general requirements (applies to all assembly and disassembly operations) Subpart CC

Crane and Derrick Safety - Subpart CC

§1926.1404 (h)(1) Assembly/Disassembly-general requirements

20. The A/D director supervising the assembly/disassembly operation must address the hazards associated with the operation, which include: *Site and ground bearing conditions*. Site and ground conditions must be adequate for safe assembly/disassembly operations and to supports the equipment during assembly/disassembly (see § 1926. ___ for ground condition requirements).
    (a) 1402
    (b) 1403(c)
    (c) 1404(a)
    (d) 1404(b)
    Answer: (a) 1402. §1926.1404(h)(1) Assembly/Disassembly-general requirements (applies to all assembly and disassembly operations). Subpart CC

§1926.1404 (h)(2) Assembly/Disassembly-general requirements

21. The A/D director supervising the assembly/disassembly operation must address the hazards associated with the operation, which include: *Blocking material*. The size, amount, condition and method of ___ the blocking must be sufficient to sustain the loads and maintain stability.
    (a) setting
    (b) stacking
    (c) spacing
    (d) aligning
    Answer: (b) stacking § 1926.1404(h)(2) Assembly/Disassembly-general requirements (applies to all assembly and disassembly operations). Subpart CC

§1926.1404 (h)(3) Assembly/Disassembly-general requirements

22. When used to support lattice booms or components, ___ must be appropriately placed to:
    (a) support
    (b) cribbing
    (c) blocking
    (d) timbers
    Answer: (c) blocking §1926.1404(h)(3) *Proper location of blocking.* Assembly/Disassembly- general requirements (applies to all assembly and disassembly operations). Subpart CC

§1926.1404 (h)(3)(i) Assembly/Disassembly-general requirements

23. When used to support lattice booms or components, blocking must be appropriately placed to: Protect the ___ of the equipment, and
    (a) integrity
    (b) structure
    (c) structural integrity
    (d) boom and ancillary parts
    Answer: (c) structural integrity §1926.1404(h)(3)(i) Assembly/Disassembly-general requirements (applies to all assembly and disassembly operations) Subpart CC

Crane and Derrick Safety - Subpart CC

§1926.1404 (h)(3)(ii) Assembly/Disassembly-general requirements

24. *Proper location of blocking.* When used to support lattice booms or components, blocking must be appropriately placed to: Protect the structural integrity of the equipment, and prevent ___ movement and collapse.
    (a) sudden
    (b) dangerous
    (c) rotational
    (d) rotation

    Answer: (b) dangerous. §1926.1404(h)(3)(ii) Assembly/Disassembly-general requirements (applies to all assembly and disassembly operations) Subpart CC

§1926.1404 (h)(4) Assembly/Disassembly-general requirements

25. *Verifying assist crane loads.* When using an assist crane, the loads the will be imposed on the assist crane at each phase of assembly/disassembly must be verified in accordance with §1926.___ before assembly/disassembly begins.
    (a) 1404(c)(1)(i)
    (b) 1417(o)(3)
    (c) 1421(g)(1)(ii)
    (d) 1492(m)(3)

    Answer: (b) 1471(o)(3). §1926.1404(h)(4) *Verifying assist crane loads.* Assembly/Disassembly - general requirements (applies to all assembly/disassembly operations) Subpart CC

§1926.1404 (h)(5) Assembly/Disassembly-general requirements

26. *Boom and jib pick points.* The point(s) of attachment of rigging to a boom (or boom sections or jib or jib sections) must be ___ for preventing structural damage and facilitating safe handling of these components.
    (a) suitable
    (b) structurally
    (c) sufficiently strong
    (d) reinforced

    Answer: (a) suitable. §1926.1404(h)(5) *Boom and jib pick points*: Assembly/Disassembly-general requirements (applies to all assembly/disassembly operations) Subpart CC

§1926.1404 (h)(6) Assembly/Disassembly-general requirements

27. 1926.1404(h)(6) discusses ___.
    (a) *Load points*
    (b) *Forces acting on crane booms*
    (c) *Center of gravity*
    (d) *Vector forces*

    Answer: (c) *Center of gravity* § 1926.1404(h)(6) Assembly/Disassembly-general requirements (applies to all assembly/disassembly operations) Subpart CC

Crane and Derrick Safety - Subpart CC

§1926.1404 (h)(6)(i) Assembly/Disassembly-general requirements
28. The center of gravity must be ___ if that is necessary for the method used for maintaining stability.
    (a) identified
    (b) determined
    (c) computed
    (d) established
    Answer: (a) identified § 1926.1404(h)(6)(i) Assembly/Disassembly-general requirements (applies to all assembly and disassembly operations). Subpart CC

§1926.1404 (h)(6)(ii) Assembly/Disassembly-general requirements
29. Where there is insufficient information to accurately identify the center of gravity, measures designed to prevent unintended dangerous movement resulting from an inaccurate ___ of the center of gravity must be used. (See Non-mandatory Appendix B of this subpart for an example.)
    (a) estimates
    (b) computations
    (c) identification
    (d) determination
    Answer: (c) identification. §1926.1404(h)(6)(ii) Assembly/Disassembly-general requirements (applies to all assembly and disassembly operations). Subpart CC

§1926.1404 (h)(7) Assembly/Disassembly-general requirements
30. *Stability upon pin removal.* The boom sections, boom suspension systems (such as gantry A-frames and jib struts), and components must be rigged or ___ to maintain stability upon removal of the pins.
    (a) braced
    (b) shored
    (c) supported
    (d) blocked
    Answer: (c) supported. §1926.1404(h)(7) *Stability upon pin removal.* Assembly/Disassembly-general requirements (applies to all assembly and disassembly operations) Subpart CC

§1926.1404 (h)(8) Assembly/Disassembly-general requirements
31. *Snagging.* Suspension ropes and pendants must not be allowed to catch on the on the boom or jib connection pins or cotter pins (including keepers and locking pins). From ___.
    (a) *Snagging*
    (b) *Sagging*
    (c) *Obstructions*
    (d) *Hazards*
    Answer: (a) *Snagging.* §1926.1404(h)(8) *Snagging* Assembly/Disassembly-general requirements (applies to all assembly and disassembly operations). Subpart CC

Crane and Derrick Safety - Subpart CC

§1926.1404 (h)(9) Assembly/Disassembly-general requirements

32. *Struck by counterweights.* The potential for unintended movement from inadequately supported counterweights and from hoisting counterweights. Is discussed in 1926___ *Struck by counterweights.*
    (a)   1404(h)(9)
    (b)   1404(h)(10)
    (c)   1404(h)(11)
    (d)   1404(h)(12)
    Answer: (a) 1404(h)(9) § 1926.1404(h)(9) Struck by counterweights. Assembly/Disassembly- general requirements (applies to all assembly and disassembly operations). Subpart CC

§1926.1404 (h)(10) Assembly/Disassembly-general requirements

33. *Boom hoist brake failure.* Each time reliance is to be placed on the boom hoist brake to prevent boom movement during assembly/disassembly, the brake ___ prior to such reliance to determine if it is sufficient to prevent boom movement.
    (a)   must be inspected
    (b)   shall be inspected
    (c)   must be checked
    (d)   must be tested
    Answer: (d) must be tested. §1926.1404(h)(10) Assembly/Disassembly-general requirements (applies to all assembly and disassembly operations). Subpart CC

§1926.1404 (h)(10) Assembly/Disassembly-general requirements

34. If it is not sufficient, a boom hoist ___, other locking device/back-up braking device, or other method of preventing dangerous movement of the boom (such as blocking or using an assist crane) from a boom hoist brake failure must be used.
    (a)   paw
    (b)   dog
    (c)   cat
    (d)   pawl
    Answer: (d) pawl. §1926.1404(h)(10) Assembly/Disassembly-general requirements (applies to all assembly and disassembly operations). Subpart CC

§1926.1404 (h)(11) Assembly/Disassembly-general requirements

35. 1926.1404(h)(11) discusses ___.
    (a)   crane stability
    (b)   loss of backward stability
    (c)   derrick stability
    (d)   overturning moment when hoisting heavy loads
    Answer: (b) loss of backward stability. §1926.1404(h)(11) Assembly/Disassembly-general requirements (applies to all assembly and disassembly operations). Subpart CC

Crane and Derrick Safety - Subpart CC

§1926.1404 (h)(11) Assembly/Disassembly-general requirements
36. *Loss of backward stability.* Backward stability before ___ the upperworks, travel, and when attaching or removing equipment components.
    (a) moving
    (b) swinging
    (c) traversing
    (d) lifting loads
    Answer: (b) swinging. §1926.1404(h)(11) Assembly/Disassembly-general requirements (applies to all assembly and disassembly operations). Subpart CC

§1926.1404 (h)(12) Assembly/Disassembly-general requirements
37. 1926.1404(h)(12) addresses ___.
    (a) *Counterweights*
    (b) *Wind speed and weather*
    (c) *Wind speed and weather. The effect of wind speed and weather on the equipment*
    (d) *Weather conditions and precautions*
    Answer: (c) *Wind speed and weather. The effect of wind speed and weather on the equipment.* §1926.1404(h)(12) Assembly/Disassembly-general requirements (applies to all assembly and disassembly operations). Subpart CC

§1926.1404 (i) [Reserved]

§1926.1404 (j) Assembly/Disassembly-general requirements
38. 1926.1404(j) discusses ___.
    (a) *Cantilevers*
    (b) *Cantilevered booms*
    (c) *Cantilevered boom sections*
    (d) *Cantilevered boom sections on cranes and derricks*
    Answer: (c) *Cantilevered boom sections.* §1926.1404 (j) Assembly/Disassembly-general requirements (applies to all assembly and disassembly operations). Subpart CC

§1926.1404 (j) Assembly/Disassembly-general requirements
39. *Cantilevered boom sections.* Manufacturer ___ on the maximum amount of boom supported only by cantilevering must not be exceeded.
    (a) specifications
    (b) restrictions
    (c) limits
    (d) limitations
    Answer: (d) limitations. §1926.1404(j) Assembly/Disassembly-general requirements (applies to all assembly and disassembly operations). Subpart CC

Crane and Derrick Safety - Subpart CC

§1926.1404 (j) Assembly/Disassembly-general requirements
40. Where these are ___, a registered professional engineer familiar with the type of equipment involved must determine in writing this ___, which must not be exceeded.
    (a) obsolete, engineering data
    (b) not available, equipment analysis
    (c) unavailable, limitation
    (d) inapplicable, limit
    Answer: (c) unavailable, limitation § 1926.1404(j) *Cantilevered boom sections* Assembly/Disassembly-general requirements (applies to all assembly and disassembly operations). Subpart CC

§1926.1404 (k) Assembly/Disassembly-general requirements
41. *Weight of components.* The weight of each component must be ___.
    (a) available
    (b) available on the jobsite
    (c) available with and in the required crane papers and specifications book
    (d) readily available
    Answer: (d) readily available. §1926.1404(k) *Weight of components* Assembly/Disassembly-general requirements (applies to all assembly and disassembly operations). Subpart CC

§1926.1404 (l) [Reserved]

§1926.1404 (m) Assembly/Disassembly-general requirements
42. 1926.1404(m) discusses ___.
    (a) *Materials*
    (b) *Materials and equipment handling*
    (c) *Components*
    (d) *Components and configurations*
    Answer: (d) *Components and configurations* § 1926.1404(m) Assembly/Disassembly-general requirements (applies to all assembly and disassembly operations). Subpart CC

§1926.1404 (m)(1) Assembly/Disassembly-general requirements
43. The selection of components, and configuration of equipment, that ___ the capacity or safe operation of the equipment must be in accordance with:
    (a) may impact
    (b) impact
    (c) affect
    (d) effect
    Answer: (c) affect. §1926.1404(m)(1) Assembly/Disassembly- general requirements (applies to all assembly and disassembly operations). Subpart CC

Crane and Derrick Safety - Subpart CC

§1926.1404 (m)(i) Assembly/Disassembly-general requirements

44. Manufacturer instructions, prohibitions, ___, and specifications. Where these are unavailable, a registered professional engineer familiar with the type of equipment involved must approve, in writing, the selection and configuration of components; or
    (a) limits
    (b) limitations
    (c) restrictions
    (d) forbidden
    Answer: (b) limitations § 1926.1404 (m)(1)(i) Assembly/Disassembly- general requirements (applies to all assembly and disassembly operations). Subpart CC

§1926.1404 (m)(ii) Assembly/Disassembly-general requirements

45. The selection of components, and configuration of the equipment, that affect the capacity or safe operation of the equipment must be in accordance with: Approved modifications that meet the requirements of § 1926.___ (Equipment modifications).
    (a) 1926.1404(m)(1)(ii)
    (b) 1926.1404(m)(2)
    (c) 1926.1404(n)
    (d) 1926.1434
    Answer: (d) 1926.1434. §1926.1404(m)(1) (ii) Assembly/Disassembly-general requirements (applies to all assembly and disassembly operations). Subpart CC

§1926.1404 (m)(2) Assembly/Disassembly-general requirements

46. *Post-assembly inspection*. Upon completion of assembly, the equipment must be inspected to ensure compliance with paragraph (__) of this section. (see §1926.1412(c) for post-assembly requirements).
    (a) 1404(i)
    (b) 1404(m)
    (c) 1404(m)(1)
    (d) 1404(m)(1)(ii)
    Answer: (c) 1404(m)(1) §1926.1404 (m)(2) *Post assembly inspection* Assembly/Disassembly- general requirements (applies to all assembly and disassembly operations) Subpart CC

§1926.1404 (n) [Reserved]

§1926.1404 (o) Assembly/Disassembly-general requirements

47. *Shipping pins*. Reusable shipping pins, straps, links, and similar equipment must be removed. Once they are removed they must either be ___ or otherwise ___ so that they will not present a falling object hazard.
    (a) scrapped, stored
    (b) salvaged, used
    (c) reinspected, discarded
    (d) stowed, stored
    Answer: (d) stowed, stored § 1926.1404(o) Shipping pins. Assembly/Disassembly-general requirements (applies to all assembly and disassembly operations) Subpart CC

Crane and Derrick Safety - Subpart CC

§1926.1404 (p) Assembly/Disassembly-general requirements
48. *Pile driving.* Equipment used for pile driving must not have a ___ attached during pile driving operations.
    (a)   cage
    (b)   lead
    (c)   hammer
    (d)   jib
    Answer: (d) jib. §1926.1404(p) *Pile driving* Assembly/Disassembly-general requirements (applies to all assembly and disassembly operations). Subpart CC

§1926.1404 (q) Assembly/Disassembly-general requirements
49. *Outriggers and stabilizers.* When the load to be handled and the operating radius require the use of ___ or ___, or at any time when outriggers or stabilizers are used, all of the following must be met (except as otherwise indicated):
    (a)   jacks, cribbing
    (b)   cribbing, pontoons
    (c)   outriggers, stabilizers
    (d)   stabilizers, outriggers
    Answer: (c) outriggers, stabilizers. §1926.1404(q) *Outriggers and stabilizers.* Assembly/Disassembly-general requirements (applies to all assembly and disassembly operations) Subpart CC

§1926.1404 (q)(1) Assembly/Disassembly-general requirements
50. The outriggers and stabilizers must be either fully extended or, if manufacturer procedures permit, ___ as specified in the load chart.
    (a)   set
    (b)   deployed
    (c)   cribbed
    (d)   extended
    Answer: (b) deployed. §1926.1404(q)(1) Assembly/Disassembly-general requirements (applies to all assembly and disassembly operations) Subpart CC

§1926.1404 (q)(2) Assembly/Disassembly-general requirements
51. The outriggers must be set to remove the equipment weight from the wheels, except for locomotive cranes (see paragraph (___) of this section use of outriggers on locomotive cranes). This provision does not apply to stabilizers.
    (a)   (q)(6)
    (b)   (q)(7)
    (c)   (q)(7)(i)
    (d)   (q)(7)(ii)
    Answer: (a) (q)(6). §1926.1404(q)(2) Assembly/Disassembly-general requirements (applies to all assembly and disassembly operations). Subpart CC

Crane and Derrick Safety - Subpart CC

§1926.1404 (q)(3) Assembly/Disassembly-general requirements
52. *Outriggers and stabilizers*. When outrigger ___ are used, the must be attached to the outriggers.
    (a) pads
    (b) base plates
    (c) shoes
    (d) floats
    Answer: (d) floats. §1926.1404(q)(3) Assembly/Disassembly-general requirements (applies to all assembly and disassembly operations). Subpart CC

§1926.1404 (q)(3) Assembly/Disassembly-general requirements
53. When stabilizer floats are used they must be attached to the ___.
    (a) stabilizers
    (b) outriggers
    (c) sponsons
    (d) hydraulic jacks
    Answer: (a) stabilizers. §1926.1404(q)(3) Assembly/Disassembly-general requirements (applies to all assembly and disassembly operations), Subpart CC

§1926.1404 (q)(4) Assembly/Disassembly-general requirements
54. Each outrigger or stabilizer must visible to the operator or to a signal person during the extension and ___.
    (a) setting
    (b) setting operation
    (c) jacking
    (d) leveling operation
    Answer: (a) setting. §1926.1404(q)(4) Assembly/Disassembly-general requirements (applies to all assembly and disassembly operations). Subpart CC

§1926.1404 (q)(5) Assembly/Disassembly-general requirements
55. §1926.1404(q)(5) states ___.
    (a) Outrigger and stabilizer setting must conform to this section.
    (b) Outrigger and stabilizer blocking must:
    (c) Outriggers and stabilizers shall be inspected prior to setting.
    (d) Ground conditions supporting outriggers and stabilizers must be inspected before setting.
    Answer: (b) Outrigger and stabilizer blocking must: §1926.1404(q)(5) Assembly/Disassembly-general requirements (applies to all assembly and disassembly operations. Subpart CC

Crane and Derrick Safety - Subpart CC

§1926.1404 (q)(5)(i) Assembly/Disassembly-general requirements
56. Outrigger and stabilizer blocking must: Meet the requirements in paragraphs (__) and (__) of this section.
    (a) (h)(i), (h)(3)
    (b) (h)(1), (h)(3)
    (c) (H -1), (H-3)
    (d) (h)(ii), (h)(iv)
    Answer: (b) (h)(1), (h)(3) § 1926.(q)(5)(i) Assembly/Disassembly-general requirements (applies to all assembly and disassembly operations). Subpart CC

§1926.1404 (q)(5)(ii) Assembly/Disassembly-general requirements
57. Outrigger and stabilizer blocking must: Be placed only under the outrigger or stabilizer float/pad of the ___ or, where the outrigger or stabilizer is designed without a ___, under the outer bearing surface of the extended outrigger or stabilizer beam.
    (a) feet, foot
    (b) jack, jack
    (c) base plate, footer
    (d) base plate, base plate
    Answer: (b) jack, jack. §1926.1404(q)(5)(ii) Assembly/Disassembly-general requirements (applies to all assembly and disassembly operations). Subpart CC

§1926.1404 (q)(6) Assembly/Disassembly-general requirements
58. For locomotive cranes, when using outriggers or stabilizers to handle loads, the manufacturer's ___ must be followed.
    (a) instructions
    (b) recommendations
    (c) procedures
    (d) specifications
    Answer: (c) procedures. §1926.1404(q)(6) Assembly/Disassembly-general requirements (applies to all assembly and disassembly operations). Subpart CC

§1926.1404 (q)(6) Assembly/Disassembly-general requirements
59. When lifting loads without using outriggers or stabilizers, the manufacturer's procedures must be met regarding ___ or ___.
    (a) truck wedges, screws
    (b) hydraulic struts, shoring
    (c) wedges, cribbing
    (d) blocking, wedging
    Answer: (a) truck wedges, screws § 1926.1404(q)(6) Assembly/Disassembly- general requirements (applies to all assembly and disassembly operations) Subpart CC

Crane and Derrick Safety - Subpart CC

§1926.1404 (r) Assembly/Disassembly-general requirements
60. *Rigging.* In addition to following the requirements in ___ and other requirements in this and other standards applicable to rigging, when rigging is used for assembly/disassembly, the employer must ensure that:
    (a) 29 CFR 1926.251
    (b) 29 CFR 1926.251(a)(i)
    (c) 29 CFR 1926.251(b)
    (d) 29 CFR 1926.1003
    Answer: (a) 29 CFR 1926.251. §1926.1404(r) *Rigging* Assembly/Disassembly-general requirements (applies to all assembly and disassembly operations). Subpart CC

61. §1926.1404(r)(1) states ___.
    (a) The rigging work shall be done by a qualified person
    (b) The rigging work is done by a qualified rigger
    (c) The rigging work shall be done by the qualified operator
    (d) The rigging work shall be done by the qualified rigger
    Answer: (b) The rigging work is done by a qualified rigger. §1926.1404(r)(1) Assembly/Disassembly-general requirements (applies to all assembly and disassembly operations). Subpart CC

§1926.1404 (r)(2) Assembly/Disassembly-general requirements
62. Synthetic slings are protected from: Abrasive, sharp or acute edges, and configurations that could cause a reduction of the sling's rated capacity, such as distortion or ___.
    (a) strains
    (b) twisting
    (c) jerk lifts
    (d) localized compression
    Answer: (d) localized compression § 1926.1404(r)(2) Assembly/Disassembly-general requirements (applies to all assembly and disassembly operations). Subpart CC

§1926.1404 (r)(2) Assembly/Disassembly-general requirements
63. Note: Requirements for protection of wire rope slings are contained in 29 CFR 1926.___.
    (a) 251(c)(6)
    (b) 251(c)(7)
    (c) 251(c)(8)
    (d) 251(c)(9)
    Answer: (d) 251(c)(9). §1926.1404(r)(2) Assembly/Disassembly- general requirements (applies to all assembly and disassembly operations). Subpart CC

Crane and Derrick Safety - Subpart CC

§1926.1404 (r)(3) Assembly/Disassembly-general requirements
64. When synthetic slings are used, the synthetic sling manufacturer's instructions, ___, specifications and recommendations must be followed.
    (a) requirements
    (b) limits
    (c) limitations
    (d) use

    Answer: (c) limitations. §1926.1404(r)(3) Assembly/Disassembly-general requirements (apply to all assembly and disassembly operations). Subpart CC

A Ficus Tree Publishing LLC. Quick Notes Page

DU VALLS
OSHA 1926 Subpart CC — Cranes and Derricks in Construction
OSHA 1926.1405 Disassembly—additional requirements for dismantling booms and jib (applies to both the use of manufacturers procedures and employer procedures).
Instructors Manual 2014 Edition
OSHA Test CC - 8

§1926.1405 Disassembly-additional requirements for dismantling of boom and jibs
1. 1926.1405 discusses ___.
    (a) Cranes & Derricks in Construction
    (b) Safety and Health Regulations for Construction
    (c) Assembly/Disassembly-general requirements (applies to all assembly and disassembly operations).
    (d) Disassembly—additional requirements for dismantling of booms and jibs
    Answer: (d) Disassembly—additional requirements for dismantling of booms and jibs (applies to both the use of manufacturer procedures and employer procedures). §1926.1405 Subpart CC

§1926.1405 Disassembly-additional requirements for dismantling of boom and jibs
2. Dismantling (*including dismantling for* ___) booms and jibs.
    (a) *changing the length of*
    (b) *repairing*
    (c) *dismantling*
    (d) *maintenance and servicing*
    Answer: (a) *changing the length of.* §1926.1405. Subpart CC

§1926.1405 (a) Disassembly
3. None of the pins in the ___ are to be removed (partly or completely) when the pendants are in tension.
    (a) boom
    (b) jib
    (c) frame
    (d) pendants
    Answer: (d) pendants. §1926.1405(a) Subpart CC

§1926.1405 (b) Disassembly
4. None of the pins (top or bottom) on boom sections located between the ___ attachment points and the crane/derrick body are to be removed (partly or completely) when the pendants are in tension.
    (a) boom
    (b) cable
    (c) jib
    (d) pendant
    Answer: (d) pendant. §1926.1405(b) Subpart CC

Crane and Derrick Safety - Subpart CC

§1926.1405 (c) Disassembly

5. None of the pins (top or bottom) on boom sections located between the ____ and the crane/derrick body are to be removed (partly or completely) when the boom is being supported by the uppermost boom section resting on the ground (or other support).
   (a) boom load connection
   (b) lower boom section
   (c) uppermost boom section
   (d) cantilevered boom section
   Answer: (c) uppermost boom section § 1926.1405(c) Subpart CC

§1926.1405 (d) Disassembly

6. None of the top pins on boom sections located on the ___ portion of the boom being removed (the portion being removed ahead of the pendant attachment points) are to be removed (partly or completely) until the ___ to be removed is fully supported.
   (a) cantilevered, cantilevered
   (b) uppermost load bearing, uppermost load bearing
   (c) working jib, working jib
   (d) load bearing, load bearing
   Answer: (a) cantilevered, cantilevered §1926.1405(d) Subpart CC

DU VALLS
OSHA 1926 Subpart CC — Cranes and Derricks in Construction
OSHA 1926.1406 Assembly/Disassembly—employer procedures — general requirements.
Instructors Manual 2014 Edition
OSHA Test CC - 9

§1926.1406 Assembly/Disassembly—employer procedures—general requirements.
1. 1926.1406(a). When using employer procedures instead of manufacturer___ for assembly/disassembly, the employer must ensure that the procedures:
   (a) procedures
   (b) instructions
   (c) guidelines
   (d) procedures and instructions
   Answer: (a) procedures. §1926.1406 (a). Subpart CC.

§1926.1406 (a)(1) Assembly/Disassembly—employer procedures—general requirements.
2. (1) Prevent ___ dangerous movement, and prevent collapse, of any part of the equipment.
   (a) unintentional
   (b) unintended
   (c) accidental
   (d) sudden
   Answer: (b) unintended. §1926.1406(a)(1) Subpart CC

§1926.1406 (a)(2) Assembly/Disassembly—employer procedures—general requirements.
3. When using employer procedures instead of manufacturer procedures for assembly/disassembly, the employer must ensure that the procedures: Provide ___ support and stability of all parts of the equipment.
   (a) sufficient
   (b) the necessary
   (c) the required
   (d) adequate
   Answer: (d) adequate § 1926.1406(a)(2) Subpart CC

§1926.1406 (a)(3) Assembly/Disassembly—employer procedures—general requirements.
4. Position employees involved in the assembly/disassembly operation so that their ___ to unintended movement or collapse of part of or all of the equipment is minimize.
   (a) location
   (b) exposure
   (c) position
   (d) exposed position
   Answer: (b) exposure §1926.1406(a)(3) Subpart CC

Crane and Derrick Safety - Subpart CC

§1926.1406 (b) Assembly/Disassembly—employer procedures—general requirements.

5. Employer procedures must be developed by a ___.
- (a) Registered engineer
- (b) qualified engineer
- (c) qualified rigger
- (d) qualified person

Answer: (d) qualified person. §1926.1406(b) Subpart CC

DU VALLS
OSHA 1926 Subpart CC — Cranes and Derricks in Construction
OSHA 1926.1407 Power line safety (up to 350kV) assembly/disassembly.
Instructors Manual 2014 Edition
OSHA Test CC - 10

§1926.1407 (a) Power line safety (up to 350kV)—assembly/disassembly

1. Before assembling or disassembling equipment, the employer must determine if any part of the equipment, load line, or load (including rigging and lifting accessories) could get, in the direction or area of assembly/disassembly, closer than ____ feet to a power line during the assembly/disassembly process.
   (a) 15
   (b) 20
   (c) 25
   (d) 28
   Answer: (b) 20 § 1926.1407(a) Subpart CC

§1926.1407 (a) Power line safety (up to 350kV)—assembly/disassembly

2. Before assembling or disassembling equipment, the employer must determine if any part of the equipment, load line, or load (including rigging and lifting accessories) could get, in the direction or areas of assembly/disassembly, closer than ____ feet to a power line during the assembly/disassembly process. If so, the employer must meet the requirements in Option (1), Option (2), or Option (3) ____.
   (a) 15, and Option (4)
   (b) 20, of this section, as follows:
   (c) 20, of this section, as follows
   (d) 25, of this section, as follows.
   Answer: (b) 20, of this section, as follows: §1926.1407(a) Subpart CC

§1926.1407 (a)(1) Power line safety (up to 350kV)—assembly/disassembly

3. Confirm from the utility owner/operator that the power line has been deenergized and visibly grounded at the worksite. From ____.
   (a) Option (1)
   (b) Option (2)
   (c) Option (3)
   (d) Option (4)
   Answer: (a) *Option (1)- Deenergize and ground.* §1926.1407(a)(1) Subpart CC

§1926.1407 (a)(2) Power line safety (up to 350kV)—assembly/disassembly

4. Ensure that no part of the equipment, load line (including rigging and lifting accessories), gets closer than 20 feet to the power line by implementing the measures specified in paragraph (____) of this section.
   (a) a
   (b) b
   (c) c
   (d) d
   Answer: (b) b § 1926.1407(a)(2) *Option (2)-20 foot clearance.* Subpart CC

Crane and Derrick Safety - Subpart CC

§1926.1407 (a)(3) Power line safety (up to 350kV)—assembly/disassembly
5. Option (3) —.
   (a) *Clearance Tables*
   (b) *Table A clearance.*
   (c) *Table 1407 - clearances*
   (d) *Table 1407 A-1 clearances*
   Answer: (b) Table A clearance. §1926.1407(a)(3) Subpart CC

§1926.1407 (a)(3)(i) Power line safety (up to 350kV)—assembly/disassembly
6. Determine the line's voltage and minimum clearance distance permitted under Table A (see___).
   (a) § 1926.1408
   (b) § 1926.1408(a)
   (c) § 1926.1409
   (d) § 1926.1410
   Answer: (a) § 1926.1408 from §1926.1407(a)(3)(i) Subpart CC

§1926.1407 (a)(3)(ii) Power line safety (up to 350kV)—assembly/disassembly
7. Determine if any part of the equipment, load line, or load (including rigging and lifting accessories), could get closer than the minimum clearance distance to the power line permitted under Table A (see___).
   (a) §1926.1408
   (b) §1926.1408(a)
   (c) §1926.1409
   (d) §1926.1410
   Answer: (a) §1926.1408 from 1926.1407(a)(3)(ii) Subpart CC

§1926.1407 (a)(3)(ii) Power line safety (up to 350kV)—assembly/disassembly
8. Determine if any part of the equipment, load line, or load (including rigging and lifting accessories), could get closer than the minimum clearance distance to the power line permitted under Table A (see §1926.1408). If so, then the employer must follow the requirements of paragraph (__) of this section to ensure that no part of the equipment, load line, or load (including rigging and lifting accessories), gets closer to the line than the minimum clearance distance.
   (a) 1926.1407(a)(1)(h)
   (b) 1926.1407 (a)(2)(i)
   (c) 1926.1407(a)(3)(ii)
   (d) 1926.1407(a)(4)(ii)
   Answer: (c) 1926.1407(a)(3)(ii) Subpart CC

Crane and Derrick Safety - Subpart CC

§1926.1407 (b) Power line safety (up to 350kV)—assembly/disassembly
9. Where encroachment precautions are required under Option (2), or Option (3) of this section, all of the following requirements must be met: From ___.
   (a) 1926.1407(a)(3)(ii)
   (b) 1926.1407(b)
   (c) 1926.1407(b)(1)(i)
   (d) 1926.1407(b)(2)(ii)
   Answer: (b) 1926.1407(b). §1926.1407(b) *Preventing encroachment/electrocution* Subpart CC

§1926.1407 (b)(1) Power line safety (up to 350kV)—assembly/disassembly
10. Where encroachment precautions are required under Option (2), or Option (3) of this section, all the following requirements must be met: Conduct a planned meeting with the Assembly/Disassembly director (A/D director), operator, assembly/disassembly crew and the other workers who will be in the assembly/disassembly area to review the location of the power line(s) and the ___ that will be implemented to prevent encroachment/electrocution.
    (a) steps
    (b) safety procedures
    (c) erection/dismantling procedures
    (d) assembly/disassembly procedures
    Answer: (a) steps §1926.1407(b)(1). Subpart CC

§1926.1407 (b)(2) Power line safety (up to 350kV)—assembly/disassembly
11. If tag lines are used they must be ___.
    (a) manila line
    (b) nonconductive
    (c) firmly attached to the load
    (d) of sufficient length to prevent the employee guiding the load from being beneath the load.
    Answer: (b) nonconductive §1926.1407(b)(2) Subpart CC

§1926.1407 (b)(3) Power line safety (up to 350kV)—assembly/disassembly
12. At least one of the following additional measures must be in place. The measure selected from this list must be effective in preventing ___. The additional measures are:
    (a) injury
    (b) accident
    (c) accidents
    (d) encroachment
    Answer: (d) encroachment §1926.1407(b)(3) Subpart CC

Crane and Derrick Safety - Subpart CC

§1926.1407 (b)(3)(i) Power line safety (up to 350kV)—assembly/disassembly
13. Use a ___ spotter who is in continuous contact with the equipment operator. The ___ spotter must:
    (a) employee as, employee
    (b) dedicated, dedicated
    (c) qualified, qualified
    (d) rigger as, rigger
    Answer: (d) dedicated, dedicated, §1926.1407(b)(3)(i) Subpart CC

§1926.1407 (b)(3)(i)(A) Power line safety (up to 350kV)—assembly/disassembly
14. The spotter must: Be equipped with a visual ___ to assist in identifying the minimum clearance distance.
    (a) aid
    (b) guide
    (c) reference
    (d) nonconductive tool
    Answer: (a) aid §1926.1407(b)(i)(A) Subpart CC

§1926.1407 (b)(3)(i)(A) Power line safety (up to 350kV)—assembly/disassembly
15. Examples of a visual aid include but are not limited to: A clearly visible line painted on the ground; a clearly visible line of stanchions; a set of clearly visible line-of-sight landmarks (such as a fence post behind the dedicated spotter and a ___ ahead of the dedicated spotter).
    (a) building corner
    (b) building line
    (c) building monument
    (d) corner post
    Answer: (a) building corner §1926.1407(b)(3)(i)(A) Subpart CC

§1926.1407 (b)(3)(i)(B) Power line safety (up to 350kV)—assembly/disassembly
16. The dedicated spotter must: Be positioned to effectively ___ the clearance distance.
    (a) view
    (b) observe
    (c) gauge
    (d) determine
    Answer: (c) gauge §1926.1407(b)(3)(i)(B) Subpart CC

§1926.1407 (b)(3)(i)(C) Power line safety (up to 350kV)—assembly/disassembly
17. The dedicated spotter must: Where necessary, use equipment that enables the dedicated spotter to ___ directly with the operator.
    (a) signal
    (b) talk
    (c) work
    (d) communicate
    Answer: (d) communicate § 1926.1407(b)(3)(i)(C) Subpart CC

Crane and Derrick Safety - Subpart CC

§1926.1407 (b)(3)(i)(D) Power line safety (up to 350kV)—assembly/disassembly
18. The dedicated spotter must: Give ___ information to the operator so that the required clearance distance can be maintained.
    (a)   quick
    (b)   important
    (c)   timely
    (d)   required
    Answer: (c) timely. §1926.1407(b)(3)(i)(D) Subpart CC

§1926.1407 (b)(3)(ii) Power line safety (up to 350kV)—assembly/disassembly
19. At least one of the following additional measures must be in place. The measure selected from this list must be effective in preventing encroachment. The additional measures are: A ____ alarm set to give the operator sufficient warning to prevent encroachment.
    (a)   proximity
    (b)   audible
    (c)   klaxon
    (d)   flashing
    Answer: (a) proximity. §1926.1407(b)(3)(ii) Subpart CC

1926.1407 (b)(3)(iii) Assembly/Disassembly Process. Subpart CC
20. The additional measures are: A device that automatically warns the operator when a ____ movement, such as a range control warning device. Such a device must be set to give the operator sufficient warning to prevent encroachment:
    (a)   blocking
    (b)   override
    (c)   danger
    (d)   stop
    Answer: (d) stop. §1926.1407(b)(3)(iii) Subpart CC

§1926.1407 (b)(3)(iv) Power line safety (up to 350kV)—assembly/disassembly
21. The additional measures are: A device that automatically limits ____ of movement, set to prevent encroachment.
    (a)   range
    (b)   speed
    (c)   direction
    (d)   extent
    Answer: (a) range. §1926.1407(b)(3)(iv) Subpart CC

§1926.1407 (b)(3)(v) Power line safety (up to 350kV)—assembly/disassembly
22. The additional measures are: An elevated warning line, barricade, or line of ____, in view of the operator, equipped with flags or similar high-visibility markings.
    (a)   signs
    (b)   posts
    (c)   range poles
    (d)   ranges
    Answer: (a) signs. §1926.1407(b)(3)(v) Subpart CC

Crane and Derrick Safety - Subpart CC

§1926.1407 (c) Power line safety (up to 350kV)—assembly/disassembly
23. No part of a crane/derrick, load line, or load (including rigging and lifting accessories), whether partially or fully assembled, is allowed below a power line unless the employer has confirmed that the utility owner/operator has deenergized and (at the worksite) visibly grounded the power line. From _____.
   (a)   1926.1407(e)
   (b)   1926.1002
   (c)   1926.1407(c)
   (d)   1926.1402
   Answer: (c) 1926.1407(c). §1926.1707(c) *Assembly/Disassembly below power lines prohibited.* Subpart CC

§1926.1407 Power line safety (up to 350kV)—assembly/disassembly
24. No part of a crane/derrick, load line, or load (including rigging and lifting accessories), whether partially or fully assembled, is allowed closer than the minimum approach distance under ___ (see § 1926.1408) to a power line unless the employer has confirmed that the utility owner/operator has deenergized and (at the worksite) visibly grounded the power line.
   (a)   Table A
   (b)   Table B
   (c)   Table C
   (d)   Table D
   Answer: (a) Table A. §1926.1407(d) *Assembly/Disassembly inside Table A clearance prohibited.* Subpart CC

§1926.1407 (e) Power line safety (up to 350kV)—assembly/disassembly
25. Where Option (3) of this section is used, the utility owner/operator of the power lines must provide the requested voltage information within ___ of the employer's request.
   (a)   24 hours
   (b)   48 hours
   (c)   two working days
   (d)   three working days
   Answer: (c) two working days §1926.1407(e) *Voltage information.* Subpart CC

§1926.1407 (f) Power line safety (up to 350kV)—assembly/disassembly
26. The employer must assume that all power lines are energized unless the utility owner/operator confirms that the power line has been and continues to be deenergized and visibly grounded at the worksite. From 1926.___.
   (a)   1407(f)
   (b)   1407(g)
   (c)   1407(h)
   (d)   1408
   Answer: (a) 1407(f) §1926.1407(f) *Power lines presumed to be energized.* Subpart CC

Crane and Derrick Safety - Subpart CC

§1926.1407 (g) Power line safety (up to 350kV)—assembly/disassembly

27. There must be at least _____ electrocution hazard warning conspicuously posted in the cab so that it is in view of the operator (except for overhead gantry and tower cranes) at least _____ on the outside of the equipment.
    (a) one, two
    (b) two, three
    (c) three, four
    (d) four, four

    Answer: (a) one, two. §1926.1407(g) *Posting of electrocution warnings.* Subpart CC

A Ficus Tree Publishing LLC. Quick Notes Page

DU VALLS
OSHA 1926 Subpart CC — Cranes and Derricks in Construction
OSHA 1926.1407 Power line safety (up to 350kV) equipment operations.
Instructors Manual 2014 Edition
OSHA Test CC - 11

§1926.1408 (a) Power line safety (up to 350kV)—Equipment operations

1. 1926.1408 (a) addresses ___.
   - (a) *Hazard assessments and precautions inside the work zone*
   - (b) *Option (1)*
   - (c) *Defining the work zone*
   - (d) *Preventing encroachment/electrocution*

   Answer: (a) *Hazard assessments and precautions inside the work zone.* §1926.1408 (a) Subpart CC

§1926.1408 (a) Power line safety (up to 350kV)—Equipment operations

2. Before beginning equipment operations the employer must: Identify the work zone by? From____.
   - (a) 1926.1408
   - (b) 1926.1408(a)
   - (c) 1926.1408(a)(i)
   - (d) 1926.1408(a)(ii)

   Answer: 1926.1408(a)(1)(i). §1926.1408 (a) *Hazard assessments and precautions inside the work zone.* Subpart CC

§1926.1408 (a)(1) Power line safety (up to 350kV)—Equipment operations

3. Identify the work zone by ___ Demarcating boundaries (such as with flags, or a ___
   - (a) either, device
   - (b) barriers. obstacle
   - (c) warning signs, taut line
   - (d) portable bollards,

   Answer: (a) either, device. §1926.1408 (a)(1) Subpart CC

§1926.1408 (a)(1) Power line safety (up to 350kV)—Equipment operations

4. Identify the work zone by ___ Demarcating boundaries (such as with flags, or a ___
   - (a) either, device
   - (b) barriers. obstacle
   - (c) warning signs, taut line
   - (d) portable bollards,

   Answer: (a) either, device §1926.1408 (a)(1) Subpart CC

Crane and Derrick Safety - Subpart CC

§1926.1408 (a)(1)(i) Power line safety (up to 350kV)—Equipment operations
5. Identify the work zone by ___ Demarcating boundaries (such as with flags, or a ___ such as a range limit device or range-control ___ device) and
   (a) either, device, warning
   (b) barriers. obstacle, limiting
   (c) warning signs, taut line, marker
   (d) portable bollards, stop
   Answer: (a) either, device, warning § 1926.1408 (a)(1)(i) Subpart CC

§1926.1408 (a)(1)(i) Power line safety (up to 350kV)—Equipment operations
6. Identify the work zone by ___ Demarcating boundaries (such as with flags, or a ___ such as a range limit device or range-control ___ device) and ___ the operator from operating the equipment past those boundaries, or
   (a) either, device, warning, prohibiting
   (b) barriers. obstacle, limiting, prohibit
   (c) warning signs, taut line, marker, limit
   (d) portable bollards, stop, forbid
   Answer: (a) either, device, warning, prohibiting. §1926.1408 (a)(1)(i) Subpart CC

§1926.1408 (a)(1)(ii) Power line safety (up to 350kV)—Equipment operations
7. Identify the work zone by ___ Demarcating boundaries (such as with flags, or a ___ such as a range limit device or range-control ___ device) and ___ the operator from operating the equipment past those boundaries, or Defining the work zone as the area 360 degrees the equipment, up to the equipment's maximum working ___.
   (a) either, device, warning, prohibiting, radius
   (b) barriers. obstacle, limiting, prohibit, range
   (c) warning signs, taut line, marker, limit, arc
   (d) portable bollards, stop, forbid, limit
   Answer: (a) either, device, warning, prohibiting, radius § 1926.1408 (a)(1)(ii) Subpart CC

§1926.1408 (a)(2) Power line safety (up to 350kV)—Equipment operations
8. (2) Determine if any part of the equipment , load line or load (including rigging and lifting accessories), if operated up to the equipment's maximum working radius in the work zone, could get closer than ___ feet to a power line.
   (a) 10
   (b) 15
   (c) 20
   (d) 25
   Answer: (c) 20. §1926.1408 (a)(2) Subpart CC

Crane and Derrick Safety - Subpart CC

§1926.1408 (a)(2) Power line safety (up to 350kV)—Equipment operations

9. (2) Determine if any part of the equipment, load line or load (including rigging and lifting accessories), if operated up to the equipment's maximum working radius in the work zone, could get closer than ___ feet to a power line. If so, the employer must meet the requirements in Option (___), Option (___), or Option (___) of this section, as follows:
   (a) 10, I, II, III
   (b) 15, a, b, c
   (c) 20, 1, 2, 3
   (d) 25, A, B, C
   Answer: (c) 20, 1, 2, 3. §1926.1408 (a)(2) Subpart CC

§1926.1408 (a)(2)(i) Power line safety (up to 350kV)—Equipment operations

10. (2) Determine if any part of the equipment, load line or load (including rigging and lifting accessories), if operated up to the equipment's maximum working radius in the work zone, could get closer than ___ feet to a power line. If so, the employer must meet the requirements in Option (1), Option (2), or Option (3) of this section, as follows:
    (i) Option (1) — ___ and ground. Confirm from the utility owner/operator that the power line has been ___ and visibly grounded at the worksite.
    (a) Disconnect, disengaged
    (b) Disengaged, disconnected
    (c) Deenergized, disengaged
    (d) Deenergize, deenergized
    Answer: (d) Deenergize, deenergized. §1926.1408 (a)(2)(i). Subpart CC

§1926.1408 (a)(2)(i) Power line safety (up to 350kV)—Equipment operations

11. (2) Determine if any part of the equipment, load line or load (including rigging and lifting accessories), if operated up to the equipment's maximum working radius in the work zone, could get closer than ___ feet to a power line. If so, the employer must meet the requirements in Option (1), Option (2), or Option (3) of this section, as follows:
    (i) Option (1) — ___ and ground. Confirm from the utility owner/operator that the power line has been ___ and visibly grounded at the worksite.
    (ii) Option (2)—20 Foot clearance. Ensure that no part of the equipment, load line, or load (including ___) gets closer than 20 feet to the power line by implementing the measures specified in paragraph (b) of this section.
    (a) Disconnect, disengaged, boom or jib
    (b) Disengaged, disconnected, boom or wire rope
    (c) Deenergized, disengaged, jib or wire rope
    (d) Deenergize, deenergized, rigging and lifting accessories
    Answer: (d) Deenergize, deenergized, rigging and lifting accessories. §1926.1408 (a)(2)(i). Subpart CC

Crane and Derrick Safety - Subpart CC

§1926.1408 (a)(2)(i) Power line safety (up to 350kV)—Equipment operations

12. (2) Determine if any part of the equipment, load line or load (including rigging and lifting accessories), if operated up to the equipment's maximum working radius in the work zone, could get closer than ___feet to a power line. If so, the employer must meet the requirements in Option (1), Option (2), or Option (3) of this section, as follows:
    (i) Option (1)— ___ and ground. Confirm from the utility owner/operator that the power line has been ___ and visibly grounded at the worksite.
    (ii) Option (2)—20 Foot clearance. Ensure that no part of the equipment, load line, or load (including ___) gets closer than 20 feet to the power line by implementing the measures specified in paragraph (b) of this section.
    (iii) Option (3)—Table ___ clearance.
    (a)   Disconnect, disengaged, boom or jib, B
    (b)   Disengaged, disconnected, boom or wire rope, C
    (c)   Deenergized, disengaged, jib or wire rope, D
    (d)   Deenergize, deenergized, rigging and lifting accessories, A
    Answer: (d) Deenergize, deenergized, rigging and lifting accessories, A.
    §1926.1408 (a)(2)(i)(ii)(iii). Subpart CC

§1926.1408 (a)(2)(i) Power line safety (up to 350kV)—Equipment operations

13. (2) Determine if any part of the equipment, load line or load (including rigging and lifting accessories), if operated up to the equipment's maximum working radius in the work zone, could get closer than ___feet to a power line. If so, the employer must meet the requirements in Option (1), Option (2), or Option (3) of this section, as follows:
    (iii) Option (3)—Table A clearance.
    (A) Determine the line's voltage and the minimum approach distance permitted under Table A (see 1926.___).
    (B) Determine if any part of the equipment, load line or load (including rigging and lifting accessories), while operating up to the equipment's maximum ___ in the work zone, could get closer than the minimum approach distance to the power line
    (a)   1406, operating radius
    (b)   1407, arc radius
    (c)   1408, working radius
    (d)   1409, swing radius
    Answer: (c) 1408, working radius. §1926.1408 (a)(2)(iii)(A)(B). Subpart CC

Crane and Derrick Safety - Subpart CC

§1926.1408 (a)(2)(i) Power line safety (up to 350kV)—Equipment operations

14. (2) Determine if any part of the equipment, load line or load (including rigging and lifting accessories), if operated up to the equipment's maximum working radius in the work zone, could get closer than ___ feet to a power line. If so, the employer must meet the requirements in Option (1), Option (2), or Option (3) of this section, as follows:
(iii) Option (3)—Table A clearance.
(A) Determine the line's voltage and the minimum approach distance permitted under Table A (see 1926.___).
(B) Determine if any part of the equipment, load line or load (including rigging and lifting accessories), while operating up to the equipment's maximum ___ in the work zone, could get closer than the minimum approach distance to the power line permitted under Table A (see §1926.___).
   (a)   1406, operating radius, 1406
   (b)   1407, arc radius, 1407
   (c)   1408, working radius, 1408
   (d)   1409, swing radius, 1409
Answer: (c) 1408, working radius, 1408. §1926.1408 (a)(2)(iii)(A)(B). Subpart CC

§1926.1408 (a)(2)(i) Power line safety (up to 350kV)—Equipment operations

15. (2) Determine if any part of the equipment, load line or load (including rigging and lifting accessories), if operated up to the equipment's maximum working radius in the work zone, could get closer than ___ feet to a power line. If so, the employer must meet the requirements in Option (1), Option (2), or Option (3) of this section, as follows:
(iii) Option (3)—Table A clearance.
(A) Determine the line's voltage and the minimum approach distance permitted under Table A (see 1926.___).
(B) Determine if any part of the equipment, load line or load (including rigging and lifting accessories), while operating up to the equipment's maximum ___ in the work zone, could get closer than the minimum approach distance to the power line permitted under Table A (see §1926.___). If so, then the employer must follow the requirements in paragraph (___) of this section to ensure that no part of the equipments, load line, or load (including rigging and lifting accessories), gets closer to the line than the minimum approach distance.
   (a)   1406, operating radius, 1406, d
   (b)   1407, arc radius, 1407, a
   (c)   1408, working radius, 1408, b
   (d)   1409, swing radius, 1409, c
Answer: (c) 1408, working radius, 1408, b. §1926.1408 (a)(2)(iii)(A)(B). Subpart CC

Crane and Derrick Safety - Subpart CC

§1926.1408 (b) Preventing encroachment/electrocution
16.   (2) Option (3)—Table A clearance. Preventing encroachment/electrocution (B)(b). Where encroachment precautions are required under Option (__) or Option (__) of this section, all of the following requirements must be met.
    - (a)   1, 2
    - (b)   2, 3
    - (c)   1, 3
    - (d)   2, 4

    Answer: (b) 2, 3. §1926.1408(B)(b) Preventing encroachment/electrocution. Subpart CC

§1926.1408 (b)(1) Preventing encroachment/electrocution
17.   (2) Option (3)—Table A clearance. Preventing encroachment/electrocution (B)(b). Where encroachment precautions are required under Option (__) or Option (__) of this section, all of the following requirements must be met.
    (1) Conduct a ___ meeting with the operator and the other workers who will be in the area of the equipment or load to review the location of the power line(s), and
    - (a)   1, 2, safety
    - (b)   2, 3, planning
    - (c)   1, 3, construction
    - (d)   2, 4, operations

    Answer: (b) 2, 3, planning. §1926.1408 (B)(b)(1) Preventing encroachment/electrocution. Subpart CC

§1926.1408 (b)(1) Preventing encroachment/electrocution
18.   (2) Option (3)—Table A clearance. Preventing encroachment/electrocution (B)(b). Where encroachment precautions are required under Option (__) or Option (__) of this section, all of the following requirements must be met.
    (1) Conduct a ___ meeting with the operator and the other workers who will be in the area of the equipment or load to review the location of the power line(s), and the steps that will be ___ to prevent encroachment/electrocution.
    - (a)   1, 2, safety, requirements
    - (b)   2, 3, planning, steps
    - (c)   1, 3, construction, procedures
    - (d)   2, 4, operations, followed

    Answer: (b) 2, 3, planning, steps. §1926.1408 (B)(b)(1) Preventing encroachment/electrocution. Subpart CC

Crane and Derrick Safety - Subpart CC

§1926.1408 (b)(1) Preventing encroachment/electrocution

19. (2) Option (3)—Table A clearance. Preventing encroachment/electrocution (B)(b). Where encroachment precautions are required under Option (___) or Option (___) of this section, all of the following requirements must be met.
    (1) Conduct a ___ meeting with the operator and the other workers who will be in the area of the equipment or load to review the location of the power line(s), and the steps that will be ___ to prevent encroachment/electrocution.
    (2) If tag lines are to be used, they ___ be non-conductive.
    (a)　　1, 2, safety, requirements, shall
    (b)　　2, 3, planning, steps, must
    (c)　　1, 3, construction, procedures, will
    (d)　　2, 4, operations, followed, must
    Answer: (b) 2, 3, planning, steps, must. §1926.1408 (b)(2)Preventing encroachment/electrocution. Subpart CC

§1926.1408 (b)(3) Preventing encroachment/electrocution

20. (3) Erect and maintain an ___ warning line, barricade, or line of signs, in view of the operator,
    (a)　　taut
    (b)　　flagged
    (c)　　elevated
    (d)　　visible
    Answer: (c) elevated. §1926.1408 (b)(3) Preventing encroachment/electrocution. Subpart CC

§1926.1408 (b)(3) Preventing encroachment/electrocution

21. (3) Erect and maintain an ___ warning line, barricade, or line of signs, in view of the operator, equipped with flags or similar high-visibility markings, at ___feet from the power line (if using Option 2 of this section) or at the minimum approach distance under Table A (see §1926.1408) (if using Option (3) of this section).
    (a)　　taut, 10
    (b)　　flagged, 15
    (c)　　elevated, 20
    (d)　　visible, 25
    Answer: (c) elevated, 20. §1926.1408 (b)(3) Preventing encroachment/electrocution. Subpart CC

Crane and Derrick Safety - Subpart CC

§1926.1408 (b)(3) Preventing encroachment/electrocution

22. (3) Erect and maintain an ___ warning line, barricade, or line of signs, in view of the operator, equipped with flags or similar high-visibility markings, at ___ feet from the power line (if using Option 2 of this section) or at the minimum approach distance under Table A (see §1926.1408) (if using Option (3) of this section). If the operator is unable to see the elevated warning line, a ___ must be used as described in
    (a) taut, 10, crane boom spotter
    (b) flagged, 15, qualified spotter
    (c) elevated, 20, dedicated spotter
    (d) visible, 25, qualified spotter
    Answer: (c) elevated, 20, dedicated spotter. §1926.1408 (b)(3) Preventing encroachment/electrocution. Subpart CC

§1926.1408 (b)(3) Preventing encroachment/electrocution

23. (3) Erect and maintain an ___ warning line, barricade, or line of signs, in view of the operator, equipped with flags or similar high-visibility markings, at ___ feet from the power line (if using Option 2 of this section) or at the minimum approach distance under Table A (see §1926.1408) (if using Option (3) of this section). If the operator is unable to see the elevated warning line, a ___ must be used as described in §1926.1408 ___ in addition to implementing one of the measures described in
    (a) taut, 10, crane boom spotter, (a)(3)(ii)
    (b) flagged, 15, qualified spotter, (b)(3)(i)
    (c) elevated, 20, dedicated spotter, (b)(4)(ii)
    (d) visible, 25, qualified spotter, (b)(5)(ii)
    Answer: (c) elevated, 20, dedicated spotter, (b)(4)(ii). §1926.1408 (b)(3) Preventing encroachment/electrocution. Subpart CC

§1926.1408 (b)(3) Preventing encroachment/electrocution

24. (3) Erect and maintain an ___ warning line, barricade, or line of signs, in view of the operator, equipped with flags or similar high-visibility markings, at ___ feet from the power line (if using Option 2 of this section) or at the minimum approach distance under Table A (see §1926.1408) (if using Option (3) of this section). If the operator is unable to see the elevated warning line, a ___ must be used as described in §1926.1408 ___ in addition to implementing one of the measures described in §§ 1926.1408(b)(4)(i), (iii), (iv) and (__).
    (a) taut, 10, crane boom spotter, (a)(3)(ii), iii
    (b) flagged, 15, qualified spotter, (b)(3)(i), iv
    (c) elevated, 20, dedicated spotter, (b)(4)(ii), v
    (d) visible, 25, qualified spotter, (b)(5)(ii), (v)
    Answer: (c) elevated, 20, dedicated spotter, (b)(4)(ii), v. §1926.1408 (b)(3) Preventing encroachment/electrocution. Subpart CC

Crane and Derrick Safety - Subpart CC

§1926.1408 (b)(4)(i) Preventing encroachment/electrocution
25. (4) Implement at least one of the following measures:
    (i) A ___ alarm set to give the operator sufficient warning to prevent encroachment.
    (a) audible
    (b) warning
    (c) flashing
    (d) proximity
    Answer: (d) proximity. §1926.1408 (b)(4) Preventing encroachment/electrocution. Subpart CC

§1926.1408 (b)(4)(ii) Preventing encroachment/electrocution
26. (4) Implement at least one of the following measures:
    (i) A ___ alarm set to give the operator sufficient warning to prevent encroachment.
    (ii) A dedicated spotter who is in ___ contact with the operator.
    (a) audible, direct
    (b) warning, telephone
    (c) flashing, constant
    (d) proximity, continuous
    Answer: (d) proximity, continuous. §1926.1408 (b)(4) Preventing encroachment/electrocution. Subpart CC

§1926.1408 (b)(4)(ii) Preventing encroachment/electrocution
27. (4) Implement at least one of the following measures:
    (i) A ___ alarm set to give the operator sufficient warning to prevent encroachment.
    (ii) A dedicated spotter who is in ___ contact with the operator. Where this measure is selected, the dedicated spotter ___:
    (a) audible, direct, shall
    (b) warning, telephone, will
    (c) flashing, constant, should
    (d) proximity, continuous, must
    Answer: (d) proximity, continuous, must. §1926.1408 (b)(4) Preventing encroachment/electrocution. Subpart CC

§1926.1408 (b)(4)(A) Preventing encroachment/electrocution
28. A dedicated spotter who is in continuous contact with the operator. Where this measure is selected, the dedicated spotter must:
    (A) Be equipped with a ___ to assist in identifying the minimum clear distance.
    (a) visual aid
    (b) telephone
    (c) flag
    (d) Stadia rod
    Answer: (a) visual aid. §1926.1408 (b)(4)(A) Preventing encroachment/electrocution. Subpart CC

Crane and Derrick Safety - Subpart CC

§1926.1408 (b)(4)(A) Preventing encroachment/electrocution
29. A dedicated spotter who is in continuous contact with the operator. Where this measure is selected, the dedicated spotter must:
(A) Be equipped with a ___ to assist in identifying the minimum clear distance. Examples of a visual aid include, but are not limited to: A clearly visible line ___ on the ground; a clearly visible line of stanchions; a set of clearly visible line-of-sight landmarks (such as a fence post behind the dedicated spotter and a building corner ahead of the dedicated spotter.
(a) visual aid, painted
(b) telephone, etched
(c) flag, marked
(d) Stadia rod, marked
Answer: (a) visual aid, painted. §1926.1408 (b)(4)(A) Preventing encroachment/electrocution. Subpart CC

§1926.1408 (b)(4)(B) Preventing encroachment/electrocution
30. A dedicated spotter who is in continuous contact with the operator. Where this measure is selected, the dedicated spotter must:
(B) Be ___ to effectively gauge the clearance distance.
(a) located
(b) positioned
(c) set
(d) posted
Answer: (b) positioned. §1926.1408 (b)(4)(B) Preventing encroachment/electrocution. Subpart CC

§1926.1408 (b)(4)(C) Preventing encroachment/electrocution
31. A dedicated spotter who is in continuous contact with the operator. Where this measure is selected, the dedicated spotter must:
(C) Where necessary, use ___ that enables the dedicated spotter to communicate directly with the operator.
(a) signals
(b) tools
(c) equipment
(d) flags
Answer: (c) equipment. §1926.1408 (b)(4)(C) Preventing encroachment/electrocution. Subpart CC

Crane and Derrick Safety - Subpart CC

§1926.1408 (b)(4)(D) Preventing encroachment/electrocution
32. A dedicated spotter who is in continuous contact with the operator. Where this measure is selected, the dedicated spotter must:
(D) Give ___ information to the operator so that the required clearance distance is maintained.
  (a) accurate
  (b) fast
  (c) quick
  (d) timely
Answer: (d) timely. §1926.1408 (b)(4)(D) Preventing encroachment/electrocution. Subpart CC

§1926.1408 (b)(4)(iii) Preventing encroachment/electrocution
33. Implement at least one of the following measures:
(iii) A device that automatically warns the operator when to stop movement, such as a ___ warning device.
  (a) range control
  (b) swing control
  (c) rotation control
  (d) proximity
Answer: (a) range control. §1926.1408 (b)(4)(iii) Preventing encroachment/electrocution. Subpart CC

§1926.1408 (b)(4)(iii) Preventing encroachment/electrocution
34. Implement at least one of the following measures:
(iii) A device that automatically warns the operator when to stop movement, such as a ___ warning device. Such a device must be set to give the operator sufficient warning to prevent ___.
  (a) range control, encroachment
  (b) swing control, contact
  (c) rotation control, exposure
  (d) proximity, contact
Answer: (a) range control, encroachment. §1926.1408 (b)(4)(iii) Preventing encroachment/electrocution. Subpart CC

§1926.1408 (b)(4)(iv) Preventing encroachment/electrocution
35. Implement at least one of the following measures:
(iv) A device that automatically limits ___, set to prevent encroachment.
  (a) range of motion
  (b) range of movement
  (c) range of rotation
  (d) boom motion
Answer: (b) range of movement. §1926.1408 (b)(4)(iv) Preventing encroachment/electrocution. Subpart CC

Crane and Derrick Safety - Subpart CC

§1926.1408 (b)(4)(v) Preventing encroachment/electrocution
36. An insulating link/device, as defined in §1926.___, installed at a point between the end of the load line (or below) and the load.
    (a) 1400
    (b) 1401
    (c) 1402
    (d) 1403
    Answer: (b) 1401. §1926.1408 (b)(4)(v) Preventing encroachment/electrocution. Subpart CC

§1926.1408 (b)(5) Preventing encroachment/electrocution
37. The requirements of paragraph (b)(4) of this section do not apply to work covered by subpart ___ of this part.
    (a) F
    (b) L
    (c) P
    (d) V
    Answer: (d) V. §1926.1408 (b)(5) Preventing encroachment/electrocution. Subpart CC

§1926.1408 (c) Voltage information
38. Where Option (3) of this section is used, the utility owner/operator of the power lines must provide the requested voltage information within ___ working days of the employer's request.
    (a) two
    (b) three
    (c) five
    (d) seven
    Answer: (a) two. §1926.1408 (c) Voltage information. Preventing encroachment/electrocution. Subpart CC

§1926.1408 (d) Operations below power lines.
39. (1) No part of the equipment, load line, or load (including rigging and lifting accessories) is allowed ___ a power line unless the employer has confirmed that the utility owner/operator has deenergized and (at the worksite) visibly grounded the power line, except
    (a) under
    (b) below
    (c) beneath
    (d) adjacent to
    Answer: (b) below. §1926.1408 (d) (1) Operations below power lines. Preventing encroachment/electrocution. Subpart CC

Crane and Derrick Safety - Subpart CC

§1926.1408 (d) Operations below power lines.
40. (1) No part of the equipment, load line, or load (including rigging and lifting accessories) is allowed ___ a power line unless the employer has confirmed that the utility owner/operator has deenergized and (at the worksite) visibly grounded the power line, except where one of the exceptions in paragraph ___ of this section applies.
    (a) under, (d)(1)
    (b) below, (d)(2)
    (c) beneath, (e)(2)
    (d) adjacent to, (e)(3)
    Answer: (b) below, (d)(2). §1926.1408 (d) (1) Operations below power lines. Preventing encroachment/electrocution. Subpart CC

§1926.1408 (d)(2) Operations below power lines.
41. (2) Exceptions. Paragraph (__) of this part is inapplicable where the employer demonstrates that one of the following applies:
    (a) (d)(1)
    (b) (d)(2)
    (c) (e)(2)
    (d) (e)(3)
    Answer: (a) (d)(1). §1926.1408 (2) (1) Exceptions. Operations below power lines. Preventing encroachment/electrocution. Subpart CC

§1926.1408 (d)(2)(i) Operations below power lines.
42. (2)(i) Exceptions. Paragraph (__) of this part is inapplicable where the employer demonstrates that one of the following applies:
    (i) The work is covered by subpart ___ of this part.
    (a) (d)(1), V
    (b) (d)(2), X
    (c) (e)(2), Y
    (d) (e)(3), Z
    Answer: (a) (d)(1), V. §1926.1408 (2) (1) Exceptions. Operations below power lines. Preventing encroachment/electrocution. Subpart CC

§1926.1408 (d)(2)(i) Operations below power lines.
43. (2)(ii) Exceptions. Paragraph (d)(1) of this part is inapplicable where the employer demonstrates that one of the following applies:
    (ii) For equipment with non-extensible booms: The uppermost part of the equipment, with the boom at true vertical, would be more than ___ feet below the plane of the power line or more than the Table A of this section minimum clearance distance below the plane of the power lines.
    (a) 15
    (b) 20
    (c) 25
    (d) 30
    Answer: (b) 20. §1926.1408 (2) (ii) Exceptions. Operations below power lines. Preventing encroachment/electrocution. Subpart CC

Crane and Derrick Safety - Subpart CC

§1926.1408 (d)(2)(iii) Operations below power lines.

44. (2)(iii) Exceptions. Paragraph (d)(1) of this part is inapplicable where the employer demonstrates that one of the following applies:
 (iii) For equipment with ___ booms or extensible booms:
 (a) multi-position
 (b) owner modified
 (c) articulating
 (d) jib
 Answer: (c) articulating. §1926.1408 (2) (iii) Exceptions. Operations below power lines. Preventing encroachment/electrocution. Subpart CC

§1926.1408 (d)(2)(iii) Operations below power lines.

45. (2)(iii) Exceptions. Paragraph (d)(1) of this part is inapplicable where the employer demonstrates that one of the following applies:
 (iii) For equipment with articulating booms or extensible booms: The uppermost part of the equipment, with the boom in the fully extended position, at the true vertical, would be 20 feet ___ the plane of the power line or more than the Table A of this section minimum clearance distance below the plane of the power line.
 (a) under
 (b) below
 (c) beneath
 (d) lower
 Answer: (b) below. §1926.1408 (2) (iii) Exceptions. Operations below power lines. Preventing encroachment/electrocution. Subpart CC

§1926.1408 (d)(2)(iv) Operations below power lines.

46. (2)(iv) Exceptions. Paragraph (d)(1) of this part is inapplicable where the employer demonstrates that one of the following applies:
 (iv) The employer demonstrates that compliance with paragraph (d)(1) of this section is infeasible and meets the requirements of §1916. ___.
 (a) 1408
 (b) 1409
 (c) 1410
 (d) 1412
 Answer: (c) 1410. §1926.1408 (2) (iv) Exceptions. Operations below power lines. Preventing encroachment/electrocution. Subpart CC

§1926.1408 (e) Power lines presumed energized.

47. (e) The employer ___ assume that all power lines are energized unless the utility owner/operator confirms that the power line has been and continues to be deenergized and is visibly grounded at the worksite.
 (a) must
 (b) shall
 (c) will
 (d) may
 Answer: (a) must. §1926.1408 (2) (iv) Exceptions. Operations below power lines. Preventing encroachment/electrocution. Subpart CC

© Copyright 2014. All rights reserved. Warning: United States Copyright Law and International Treaties prohibit unauthorized publication, distribution and reproduction of the whole, part, portion of this Work. Unauthorized use of this copyright in any form, format, sequence or document may result in severe criminal and civil penalties. Violations of this copyright are investigated by the United States Department of Justice and carry, upon conviction of fines up to $250,000 and five years confinement.
A Ficus Tree Publishing LLC., Educational - Technical Publication

Crane and Derrick Safety - Subpart CC

§1926.1408 (f) When working near transmitter/communication towers.
48. (f) When working near transmitter/communication towers where the equipment is close enough for an electrical charge to be ___ in the equipment or materials being handled, the transmitter must be deenergized or the following precautions must be taken:
(a) indicted
(b) inducted
(c) induced
(d) introduced
Answer: (c) inducted. §1926.1408 (f). When working near transmitter/communication towers. Preventing encroachment/electrocution. Subpart CC

§1926.1408 (f)(1) When working near transmitter/communication towers.
49. (f)(1) When working near transmitter/communication towers where the equipment is close enough for an electrical charge to be ___ in the equipment or materials being handled, the transmitter must be deenergized or the following precautions must be taken: (1) the electrical equipment must be provided with an ___ ground
(a) indicted, neutral
(b) inducted, negative
(c) induced, electrical
(d) introduced, positive
Answer: (c) inducted, electrical. §1926.1408 (f). When working near transmitter/communication towers. Preventing encroachment/electrocution. Subpart CC

§1926.1408 (f)(1) When working near transmitter/communication towers.
50. (f)(1) When working near transmitter/communication towers where the equipment is close enough for an electrical charge to be induced in the equipment or materials being handled, the transmitter must be deenergized or the following precautions must be taken: (1) the electrical equipment must be provided with an electrical ground (2) If tag lines are used, they ___ be non-conductive.
(a) must
(b) shall
(c) will
(d) should
Answer: (a) must. §1926.1408 (f). When working near transmitter/communication towers. Preventing encroachment/electrocution. Subpart CC

Crane and Derrick Safety - Subpart CC

§1926.1408 (g)Training.
51. (g)(1)(A) The employer must train each operator and crew member assigned to work with the equipment on all of the following:
(i) The procedures to be followed in the event of electrical contact with a power line. Such training must include:
(A) Information regarding the danger of electrocution from the operation simultaneously touching the equipment and the ___.
(a) hot leg
(b) ground
(c) wire
(d) wires
Answer: (b) ground. §1926.1408 (g). Training. Preventing encroachment/electrocution. Subpart CC

§1926.1408 (g)Training.
52. (g)(1)(B) The employer must train each operator and crew member assigned to work with the equipment on all of the following:
(i) The procedures to be followed in the event of electrical contact with a power line. Such training must include:
(B) The importance to the operator's safety of remaining inside the cab except where there is an imminent danger of fire, ___, or other emergency that necessitates leaving the cab.
(a) serious injury
(b) personal danger
(c) explosion
(d) endangerment
Answer: (c) explosion. §1926.1408 (g). Training. Preventing encroachment/electrocution. Subpart CC

§1926.1408 (g)Training.
53. (g)(1)(C) The employer must train each operator and crew member assigned to work with the equipment on all of the following:
(i) The procedures to be followed in the event of electrical contact with a power line. Such training must include:
(C) The safest way of ___ from equipment that may be energized.
(a) avoiding electrocution
(b) getting off
(c) leaving
(d) evacuating
Answer: (d) evacuating. §1926.1408 (g). Training. Preventing encroachment/electrocution. Subpart CC

Crane and Derrick Safety - Subpart CC

§1926.1408 (g)Training.

54. (g)(1)(D) The employer must train each operator and crew member assigned to work with the equipment on all of the following:
    (i) The procedures to be followed in the event of electrical contact with a power line. Such training must include:
    (D) The danger of the ___ energized zone around the equipment (step potential).
    (a) potentially
    (b) possibly
    (c) dangerous
    (d) deadly
    Answer: (a) potentially. §1926.1408 (g). Training. Preventing encroachment/electrocution. Subpart CC

§1926.1408 (g)Training.

55. (g)(1)(E) The employer must train each operator and crew member assigned to work with the equipment on all of the following:
    (i) The procedures to be followed in the event of electrical contact with a power line. Such training must include:
    (E) The need for crew in the area to avoid approaching or touching the ___ and the load.
    (a) crane
    (b) derrick
    (c) crane or derrick
    (d) equipment
    Answer: (d) equipment. §1926.1408 (g). Training. Preventing encroachment/electrocution. Subpart CC

§1926.1408 (g)Training.

56. (g)(1)(F) Safe Clearance distance from power lines.
    (ii) Power lines are presumed to be energized unless the utility owner/operator confirms that the power line has been and continues to be deenergized and ___ grounded at the worksite.
    (a) visibly
    (b) clearly
    (c) adequately
    (d) sufficiently
    Answer: (a) visibly. §1926.1408 (g). Training. Preventing encroachment/electrocution. Subpart CC

Crane and Derrick Safety - Subpart CC

§1926.1408 (g)Training.

57. (g)(1)(F) Safe Clearance distance from power lines.
(iii) Power lines are presumed to be uninsulated unless the utility owner/operator or a registered engineer who is a ___ with respect to electrical power transmission and distribution confirms that the line is insulated.
   (a)   electrical engineer
   (b)   qualified person
   (c)   qualified engineer
   (d)   operating engineer
   Answer: (b) qualified person. §1926.1408 (g). Training. Preventing encroachment/electrocution. Subpart CC

§1926.1408 (g)Training.

58. (g)(1)(F) Safe Clearance distance from power lines.
(iv) The limitations of an insulating link/device, proximity alarm, and ___ control (and similar) device, if used.
   (a)   limit
   (b)   line
   (c)   current
   (d)   range
   Answer: (d) range. §1926.1408 (g). Training. Preventing encroachment/electrocution. Subpart CC

§1926.1408 (g)Training.

59. (g)(1)(F) Safe Clearance distance from power lines.
(v) The procedures to be followed to properly ground equipment and the ___ of grounding.
   (a)   limit
   (b)   limits
   (c)   limitations
   (d)   restrictions
   Answer: (c) limitations. §1926.1408 (g). Training. Preventing encroachment/electrocution. Subpart CC

§1926.1408 (g)Training.

60. (g)(2)(F) Safe Clearance distance from power lines.
(2) Employees working as dedicated spotters must be trained to enable them to effectively perform their task, including training on the ___ requirements of this section.
   (a)   basic
   (b)   general
   (c)   applicable
   (d)   applied
   Answer: (c) applicable. §1926.1408 (g). Training. Preventing encroachment/electrocution. Subpart CC

Crane and Derrick Safety - Subpart CC

§1926.1408 (g)Training.
61. (g)(2)(F) Safe Clearance distance from power lines.
    (3) Training under this section must be administered in accordance with §1926.___.
    (a) 1430(g)
    (b) 1431(g)
    (c) 1433(h)
    (d) 1434(h)
    Answer: (a) 1430(g). §1926.1408 (g). Training. Preventing encroachment/electrocution. Subpart CC

§1926.1408 (h) Devices originally designed by nthe manufacturer for use as:
62. (h) Devices originally designed by the manufacturer for use as: A safety device (see §1926.___), operational aid, or a means to prevent power line contact or electrocution, when used to comply with this section, must meet manufacturer's procedures for use and conditions of use.
    (a) 1414
    (b) 1415
    (c) 1416
    (d) 1417
    Answer: (b) 1415. §1926.1408 (h). Training. Preventing encroachment/electrocution. Subpart CC

A Ficus Tree Publishing LLC. Quick Notes Page

DU VALLS
OSHA 1926 Subpart CC — Cranes and Derricks in Construction
OSHA 1926.1408 Power line safety (up to 350kV)
Table A—Minimum Clearance Distances
Instructors Manual 2014 Edition
OSHA Test CC - 12

§1926.1408 Power line safety (up to 350kV)—Table A—Minimum Clearance Distances

1. Voltage (nominal, kV alternating current) up to 50. The Minimum clearance distance required in (feet) = ___.
   - (a) 10
   - (b) 15
   - (c) 20
   - (d) 25

   Answer: (a) 10. §1926.1408 Table A. Subpart CC

§1926.1408 Power line safety (up to 350kV)—Table A—Minimum Clearance Distances

2. Voltage (nominal, kV alternating current) over 50 to 200. The Minimum clearance distance required in (feet) = ___.
   - (a) 10
   - (b) 15
   - (c) 20
   - (d) 25

   Answer: (b) 15. §1926.1408 Table A. Subpart CC

§1926.1408 Power line safety (up to 350kV)—Table A—Minimum Clearance Distances

3. Voltage (nominal, kV alternating current) over 200 to 350. The Minimum clearance distance required in (feet) = ___.
   - (a) 10
   - (b) 15
   - (c) 20
   - (d) 25

   Answer: (c) 20. §1926.1408 Table A. Subpart CC

§1926.1408 Power line safety (up to 350kV)—Table A—Minimum Clearance Distances

4. Voltage (nominal, kV alternating current) over 350 to 500. The Minimum clearance distance required in (feet) = ___.
   - (a) 10
   - (b) 15
   - (c) 20
   - (d) 25

   Answer: (d) 25. §1926.1408 Table A. Subpart CC

© Copyright 2014. All rights reserved. Warning: United States Copyright Law and International Treaties prohibit unauthorized publication, distribution and reproduction of the whole, part, portion of this Work. Unauthorized use of this copyright in any form, format, sequence or document may result in severe criminal and civil penalties. Violations of this copyright are investigated by the United States Department of Justice and carry, upon conviction of fines up to $250,000 and five years confinement.
A Ficus Tree Publishing LLC., Educational - Technical Publication

Subpart CC

§1926.1408 Power line safety (up to 350kV)—Table A—Minimum Clearance Distances
5. Voltage (nominal, kV alternating current) over 350 to 500. The Minimum clearance distance required in (feet) = ___.
    (a) 10
    (b) 15
    (c) 20
    (d) 25
    Answer: (d) 25. §1926.1408 Table A. Subpart CC

§1926.1408 Power line safety (up to 350kV)—Table A—Minimum Clearance Distances
6. Voltage (nominal, kV alternating current) over 500 to 750. The Minimum clearance distance required in (feet) = ___.
    (a) 25
    (b) 35
    (c) 45
    (d) over 1,000
    Answer: (b) 35. §1926.1408 Table A. Subpart CC

§1926.1408 Power line safety (up to 350kV)—Table A—Minimum Clearance Distances
7. Voltage (nominal, kV alternating current) over 750 to 1,000. The Minimum clearance distance required in (feet) = ___.
    (a) 25
    (b) 35
    (c) 45
    (d) over 1,000
    Answer: (c) 45. §1926.1408 Table A. Subpart CC

§1926.1408 Power line safety (up to 350kV)—Table A—Minimum Clearance Distances
8. Voltage (nominal, kV alternating current) over 1,000. The Minimum clearance distance required in (feet) (as established by the utility owner/operator or registered professional engineer who is a qualified person with respect to electrical power ___ and distribution).
    (a) generation
    (b) transmission
    (c) development
    (d) grids
    Answer: (b) transmission. §1926.1408 Table A. Subpart CC

Note: The value that follows "to" is up to and includes that value. For example, over 50 to 200 means up to and including 200kV.

DU VALLS
OSHA 1926 Subpart CC — Cranes and Derricks in Construction
OSHA 1926.1409 Power line safety (over 350kV)
Instructors Manual 2014 Edition
OSHA Test CC - 13

§1926.1409 Power line safety (over 350 kV).
1. The requirements of §1926.1407 and §1926.1408 apply to power lines over 350 kV except:
   (a) For power lines at or below 1000 kV, where the distance "20 feet" is specified, the distance "___feet" must be substituted; and
   (a) 30
   (b) 40
   (c) 50
   (d) 60
   Answer: (c) 50. §1926.1409 Power line safety (over 350 kV). Subpart CC.

§1926.1409 Power line safety (over 350 kV).
2. The requirements of §1926.1407 and §1926.1408 apply to power lines over 350 kV except:
   (b) For power lines over 1000 kV, the minimum clearance distance ___ be established by the utility owner/operator or registered professional engineer who is a qualified person with respect to electrical power transmission and distribution.
   (a) should
   (b) shall
   (c) must
   (d) may
   Answer: (c) must. §1926.1409 Power line safety (over 350 kV). Subpart CC.

A Ficus Tree Publishing LLC. Quick Notes Page.

DU VALLS
OSHA 1926 Subpart CC — Cranes and Derricks in Construction
OSHA 1926.1410 Power line safety (all voltages)—
Equipment operations closer than the Table A zone.
Instructors Manual 2014 Edition
OSHA Test CC - 14

§1926.1410 Power line safety (all voltages).

1. Equipment operations in which any part of the equipment, load line, or load (including rigging and lifting accessories) is closer than the minimum approach distance under Table A of §1926.1408 to an energized power line is ___, except where the employer demonstrates that all of the following requirements are met:
   - (a) disallowed
   - (b) forbidden
   - (c) prohibited
   - (d) illegal

   Answer: (c) prohibited. §1926.1410 Power line safety (all voltages). Subpart CC.

§1926.1410 (a) Power line safety (all voltages).

2. Equipment operations in which any part of the equipment, load line, or load (including rigging and lifting accessories) is closer than the minimum approach distance under Table A of §1926.1408 to an energized power line is prohibited, except where the employer demonstrates that all of the following requirements are met:
   (a) The employer determines that it is ___ to do the work without breaching the minimum approach distance under Table A of §1926.1408.
   - (a) intractable
   - (b) infeasible
   - (c) impossible
   - (d) impracticable

   Answer: (b) infeasible. §1926.1410 Power line safety (all voltages). Subpart CC.

§1926.1410 (b) Power line safety (all voltages).

3. Equipment operations in which any part of the equipment, load line, or load (including rigging and lifting accessories) is closer than the minimum approach distance under Table A of §1926.1408 to an energized power line is prohibited, except where the employer demonstrates that all of the following requirements are met:
   (b) The employer determines that, after ___ with the utility owner/operator, it is ___ to deenergize and ground the power line or relocate the power line.
   - (a) intractable
   - (b) infeasible
   - (c) impossible
   - (d) impracticable

   Answer: (b) infeasible. §1926.1410 Power line safety (all voltages). Subpart CC.

Subpart CC

§1926.1410 (c) (1) Power line safety (all voltages).
4. Equipment operations in which any part of the equipment, load line, or load (including rigging and lifting accessories) is closer than the minimum approach distance under Table A of §1926.1408 to an energized power line is prohibited, except where the employer demonstrates that all of the following requirements are met:
(c) *Minimum clearance distance.*
(1) The power line owner/operator or registered professional engineer who is a qualified person with respect to electrical power transmission and distribution determines the minimum clearance distance that must be maintained to prevent electrical contact ___ of the on-site conditions.
(a)   in light
(b)   infeasible
(c)   in view
(d)   in retrospect
Answer: (a) in light. §1926.1410 (c)(1) Power line safety (all voltages). Subpart CC.

§1926.1410 (c) (1) Power line safety (all voltages).
5. Equipment operations in which any part of the equipment, load line, or load (including rigging and lifting accessories) is closer than the minimum approach distance under Table A of §1926.1408 to an energized power line is prohibited, except where the employer demonstrates that all of the following requirements are met:
(c) *Minimum clearance distance.*
(1) The power line owner/operator or registered professional engineer who is a qualified person with respect to electrical power transmission and distribution determines the minimum clearance distance that must be maintained to prevent electrical contact ___ of the on-site conditions. The factors that must be considered in making this decision include, but are not limited to: Conditions affecting ___ conductivity; time necessary to bring the equipment, load line, and load (including rigging and lifting accessories) to a complete stop; wind conditions; degree of
(a)   in light, atmospheric
(b)   infeasible, static
(c)   in view, normal
(d)   in retrospect, abnormal
Answer: (a) in light. §1926.1410 (c)(1) Power line safety (all voltages). Subpart CC.

Subpart CC

§1926.1410 (c) (1) Power line safety (all voltages).

6. Equipment operations in which any part of the equipment, load line, or load (including rigging and lifting accessories) is closer than the minimum approach distance under Table A of §1926.1408 to an energized power line is prohibited, except where the employer demonstrates that all of the following requirements are met:
(c) *Minimum clearance distance.*
(1) The power line owner/operator or registered professional engineer who is a qualified person with respect to electrical power transmission and distribution determines the minimum clearance distance that must be maintained to prevent electrical contact ___ of the on-site conditions. The factors that must be considered in making this decision include, but are not limited to: Conditions affecting ___ conductivity; time necessary to bring the equipment, load line, and load (including rigging and lifting accessories) to a complete stop; wind conditions; degree of ___ in the power line; lighting conditions, and other conditions affecting the ability to prevent electrical contact.
  (a)   in light, atmospheric, sway
  (b)   infeasible, static, movement
  (c)   in view, normal, whipping
  (d)   in retrospect, abnormal, raveling
Answer: (a) in light, atmospheric, sway. §1926.1410 (c)(1) Power line safety (all voltages). Subpart CC.

§1926.1410 (c)(2) Power line safety (all voltages).

7. Equipment operations in which any part of the equipment, load line, or load (including rigging and lifting accessories) is closer than the minimum approach distance under Table A of §1926.1408 to an energized power line is prohibited, except where the employer demonstrates that all of the following requirements are met:
(c) *Minimum clearance distance.*
(2) Paragraph ___ of this section does not apply to work covered by subpart V of this part;
  (a)   (a)(1)
  (b)   (b)(1)
  (c)   (c)(1)
  (d)   (d)(1)
Answer: (c) (c)(1). §1926.1410 (c)(2) Power line safety (all voltages). Subpart CC.

Subpart CC

§1926.1410 Power line safety (all voltages).

8. Equipment operations in which any part of the equipment, load line, or load (including rigging and lifting accessories) is closer than the minimum approach distance under Table A of §1926.1408 to an energized power line is prohibited, except where the employer demonstrates that all of the following requirements are met:
(c) *Minimum clearance distance.*
(2) Paragraph ___ of this section does not apply to work covered by subpart V of this part; Instead, for such work, the minimum clearance distances specified in §1926.___ Table V-1 where both the requirements of this section and §1926.952(c)(3)(i) or (ii) are met.
(a) (a)(1), 948
(b) (b)(1), 949
(c) (c)(1), 950
(d) (d)(1), 952

Answer: (c) (c)(1), 950. §1926.1410 (c)(2) Power line safety (all voltages). Subpart CC.

§1926.1410 Power line safety (all voltages).

9. Equipment operations in which any part of the equipment, load line, or load (including rigging and lifting accessories) is closer than the minimum approach distance under Table A of §1926.1408 to an energized power line is prohibited, except where the employer demonstrates that all of the following requirements are met:
(d) A planning meeting with the employer and the utility owner/operator (or registered professional engineer who is a qualified person with respect to electrical power transmission and distribution) is held to determine the ___ that will be followed to prevent electrical contact and electrocution.
(a) plans
(b) requirements
(c) steps
(d) procedures

Answer: (d) procedures. §1926.1410 (d) Power line safety (all voltages). Subpart CC.

§1926.1410 (d) Power line safety (all voltages).

10. Equipment operations in which any part of the equipment, load line, or load (including rigging and lifting accessories) is closer than the minimum approach distance under Table A of §1926.1408 to an energized power line is prohibited, except where the employer demonstrates that all of the following requirements are met:
(d) A planning meeting with the employer and the utility owner/operator (or registered professional engineer who is a qualified person with respect to electrical power transmission and distribution) is held to determine the ___ that will be followed to prevent electrical contact and electrocution.
(a) plans
(b) requirements
(c) steps
(d) procedures

Answer: (d) procedures. §1926.1410 (d) Power line safety (all voltages). Subpart CC.

Subpart CC

§1926.1410 (d) Power line safety (all voltages).
11. Equipment operations in which any part of the equipment, load line, or load (including rigging and lifting accessories) is closer than the minimum approach distance under Table A of §1926.1408 to an energized power line is prohibited, except where the employer demonstrates that all of the following requirements are met:
(d) A planning meeting with the employer and the utility owner/operator (or registered professional engineer who is a qualified person with respect to electrical power transmission and distribution) is held to determine the ___ that will be followed to prevent electrical contact and electrocution.
(1) If the power line is equipped with a device that automatically reenergizes the circuit in the event of a power line contact, before the work begins, the automatic reclosing feature of the circuit interrupting device must ___ if the design of the device permits.
(a) plans, be isolated or blocked
(b) requirements, be disabled
(c) steps, be blocked off
(d) procedures, be made inoperative
Answer: (d) procedures, be made inoperative. §1926.1410 (d) Power line safety (all voltages). Subpart CC.

§1926.1410 (d) Power line safety (all voltages).
12. Equipment operations in which any part of the equipment, load line, or load (including rigging and lifting accessories) is closer than the minimum approach distance under Table A of §1926.1408 to an energized power line is prohibited, except where the employer demonstrates that all of the following requirements are met:
(d) A planning meeting with the employer and the utility owner/operator (or registered professional engineer who is a qualified person with respect to electrical power transmission and distribution) is held to determine the procedures that will be followed to prevent electrical contact and electrocution.
(2) A dedicated spotter who is in ___ contact with the operator. The dedicated spotter must:
(2)(i) Be equipped with a ___ to assist in identifying the minimum clearance distance.
(a) direct, measuring device
(b) visual, range finder
(c) radio, battery powered telephone
(d) continuous, visual aid
Answer: (d) continuous, visual aid. §1926.1410 (d) Power line safety (all voltages). Subpart CC.

Subpart CC

§1926.1410 (d)(2)(i) Power line safety (all voltages).
13. Equipment operations in which any part of the equipment, load line, or load (including rigging and lifting accessories) is closer than the minimum approach distance under Table A of §1926.1408 to an energized power line is prohibited, except where the employer demonstrates that all of the following requirements are met:
(d) A planning meeting with the employer and the utility owner/operator (or registered professional engineer who is a qualified person with respect to electrical power transmission and distribution) is held to determine the procedures that will be followed to prevent electrical contact and electrocution.
   (2)   A dedicated spotter who is in ___ contact with the operator. The dedicated spotter must:
(2)(i) Be equipped with a ___ to assist in identifying the minimum clearance distance. Examples of a visual aid include, but are not limited to: A line painted on the ground; a clearly visible line of stanchions; a set of clearly visible line-of-sight landmarks (such as a fence post behind the dedicated spotter and a ___ ahead of the dedicated spotter).
   (a)   direct, measuring device, a surveyors range pole
   (b)   visual, range finder, any large vertical object
   (c)   radio, battery powered telephone, telephone pole
   (d)   continuous, visual aid, building corner
Answer: (d) continuous, visual aid, building corner. §1926.1410 (d)(i) Power line safety (all voltages). Subpart CC.

§1926.1410 (d)(2)(ii) Power line safety (all voltages).
14. Equipment operations in which any part of the equipment, load line, or load (including rigging and lifting accessories) is closer than the minimum approach distance under Table A of §1926.1408 to an energized power line is prohibited, except where the employer demonstrates that all of the following requirements are met:
(d) A planning meeting with the employer and the utility owner/operator (or registered professional engineer who is a qualified person with respect to electrical power transmission and distribution) is held to determine the procedures that will be followed to prevent electrical contact and electrocution.
   (2)   A dedicated spotter who is in continuous contact with the operator. The dedicated spotter must:
   (ii)   Be positioned to ___ gauge the clearance distance.
   (a)   effectively
   (b)   accurately
   (c)   visually
   (d)   continuous
Answer: (a) effectively. §1926.1410 (d)(2)(ii) Power line safety (all voltages). Subpart CC.

Subpart CC

§1926.1410 (d)(2)(iii) Power line safety (all voltages).
15. Equipment operations in which any part of the equipment, load line, or load (including rigging and lifting accessories) is closer than the minimum approach distance under Table A of §1926.1408 to an energized power line is prohibited, except where the employer demonstrates that all of the following requirements are met:
(d) A planning meeting with the employer and the utility owner/operator (or registered professional engineer who is a qualified person with respect to electrical power transmission and distribution) is held to determine the procedures that will be followed to prevent electrical contact and electrocution.
- (2) A dedicated spotter who is in continuous contact with the operator. The dedicated spotter must:
- (iii) Where necessary, use equipment that ___ the dedicated spotter to communicate directly with the operator.
- (a) allows
- (b) enables
- (c) provides
- (d) permits

Answer: (b) enables. §1926.1410 (d)(2)(iii) Power line safety (all voltages). Subpart CC.

§1926.1410 (d)(2)(iv) Power line safety (all voltages).
16. Equipment operations in which any part of the equipment, load line, or load (including rigging and lifting accessories) is closer than the minimum approach distance under Table A of §1926.1408 to an energized power line is prohibited, except where the employer demonstrates that all of the following requirements are met:
(d) A planning meeting with the employer and the utility owner/operator (or registered professional engineer who is a qualified person with respect to electrical power transmission and distribution) is held to determine the procedures that will be followed to prevent electrical contact and electrocution.
- (2) A dedicated spotter who is in continuous contact with the operator. The dedicated spotter must:
- (iv) Give ___ information to the operator so that the required clearance distance can be maintained.
- (a) quickly
- (b) immediately
- (c) timely
- (d) without delay

Answer: (c) timely. §1926.1410 (d)(2)(iv) Power line safety (all voltages). Subpart CC.

Subpart CC

§1926.1410 (d)(3) Power line safety (all voltages).
17. Equipment operations in which any part of the equipment, load line, or load (including rigging and lifting accessories) is closer than the minimum approach distance under Table A of §1926.1408 to an energized power line is prohibited, except where the employer demonstrates that all of the following requirements are met:
(d) A planning meeting with the employer and the utility owner/operator (or registered professional engineer who is a qualified person with respect to electrical power transmission and distribution) is held to determine the procedures that will be followed to prevent electrical contact and electrocution.
   (3) An elevated warning line, or barrier (not attached to the crane), in view of the operator (either directly or ___ equipment), equipped with flags or similar high-visibility markings, to prevent electrical contact. However, that provision does not apply to work covered by subpart V of this part.
   (a) through video
   (b) through electronic
   (c) with electronic
   (d) with other
Answer: (a) through video. §1926.1410 (d)(3) Power line safety (all voltages). Subpart CC.

§1926.1410 (d)(4) Power line safety (all voltages).
18. Equipment operations in which any part of the equipment, load line, or load (including rigging and lifting accessories) is closer than the minimum approach distance under Table A of §1926.1408 to an energized power line is prohibited, except where the employer demonstrates that all of the following requirements are met:
(d) A planning meeting with the employer and the utility owner/operator (or registered professional engineer who is a qualified person with respect to electrical power transmission and distribution) is held to determine the procedures that will be followed to prevent electrical contact and electrocution.
   (4) *Insulating link/device.*
(i) A insulating link/device installed at a point between the end of the ___ (or below) and the load.
   (a) wire rope
   (b) cable
   (c) line
   (d) load line
Answer: (d) load line. §1926.1410 (d)(4)(i) Power line safety (all voltages). Subpart CC.

Subpart CC

§1926.1410 (d)(4) Power line safety (all voltages).
19. Equipment operations in which any part of the equipment, load line, or load (including rigging and lifting accessories) is closer than the minimum approach distance under Table A of §1926.1408 to an energized power line is prohibited, except where the employer demonstrates that all of the following requirements are met:

(d) A planning meeting with the employer and the utility owner/operator (or registered professional engineer who is a qualified person with respect to electrical power transmission and distribution) is held to determine the procedures that will be followed to prevent electrical contact and electrocution.

(4) *Insulating link/device.*

(ii) For work covered by subpart V of this part, the requirement in paragraph (d)(4)(i) of this section applies only when working inside the §___ Table V-1 clearance distances.

(a) 1926.950
(b) 1926.950 (a)
(c) 1926.950 (b)
(d) 1926.950 (c)

Answer: (a) 1926.950. §1926.1410 (d)(4)(ii) Power line safety (all voltages). Subpart CC.

§1926.1410 (d)(4)(iii) Power line safety (all voltages).
20. Equipment operations in which any part of the equipment, load line, or load (including rigging and lifting accessories) is closer than the minimum approach distance under Table A of §1926.1408 to an energized power line is prohibited, except where the employer demonstrates that all of the following requirements are met:

(d) A planning meeting with the employer and the utility owner/operator (or registered professional engineer who is a qualified person with respect to electrical power transmission and distribution) is held to determine the procedures that will be followed to prevent electrical contact and electrocution.

(4) *Insulating link/device.*

(iii) For work covered by subpart V of this part involving operations where the use of an insulating link/device is ___, the requirements of §1910.269(p)(4)(iii)(B) or (C) may be substituted for the requirement in (d)(4)(i) of this section.

(a) impracticable
(b) infeasible
(c) impossible
(d) useless

Answer: (b) infeasible. §1926.1410 (d)(4)(iii) Power line safety (all voltages). Subpart CC.

Subpart CC

§1926.1410 (d)(4)(iv) Power line safety (all voltages).

21. Equipment operations in which any part of the equipment, load line, or load (including rigging and lifting accessories) is closer than the minimum approach distance under Table A of §1926.1408 to an energized power line is prohibited, except where the employer demonstrates that all of the following requirements are met:
    (d) A planning meeting with the employer and the utility owner/operator (or registered professional engineer who is a qualified person with respect to electrical power transmission and distribution) is held to determine the procedures that will be followed to prevent electrical contact and electrocution.
    (4) *Insulating link/device.*
    (iv) Until November 8, 2011, the following procedure may be substituted for the requirements in paragraph ___ of this section:
    (a) (d)(3)
    (b) (d)(4)
    (c) (d)(4)(i)
    (d) (d)(4)(ii)
    Answer: (c) (d)(4)(i). §1926.1410 (d)(4)(iv) Power line safety (all voltages). Subpart CC.

§1926.1410 (d)(4)(iv) Power line safety (all voltages).

22. Equipment operations in which any part of the equipment, load line, or load (including rigging and lifting accessories) is closer than the minimum approach distance under Table A of §1926.1408 to an energized power line is prohibited, except where the employer demonstrates that all of the following requirements are met:
    (d) A planning meeting with the employer and the utility owner/operator (or registered professional engineer who is a qualified person with respect to electrical power transmission and distribution) is held to determine the procedures that will be followed to prevent electrical contact and electrocution.
    (4) *Insulating link/device.*
    (iv) Until November 8, 2011, the following procedure may be substituted for the requirements in paragraph ___ of this section: All employees, excluding equipment operators located on the equipment, who may come in contact with the equipment load line, or the load must be insulated or guarded from the equipment, the load line, and ___.
    (a) (d)(3), the lift
    (b) (d)(4), the hoisting equipment
    (c) (d)(4)(i), the load
    (d) (d)(4)(ii), the hosting equipment and accessories
    Answer: (c) (d)(4)(i), the load. §1926.1410 (d)(4)(iv) Power line safety (all voltages). Subpart CC.

Subpart CC

§1926.1410 (d)(4)(iv) Power line safety (all voltages).
23. Equipment operations in which any part of the equipment, load line, or load (including rigging and lifting accessories) is closer than the minimum approach distance under Table A of §1926.1408 to an energized power line is prohibited, except where the employer demonstrates that all of the following requirements are met:

    (d) A planning meeting with the employer and the utility owner/operator (or registered professional engineer who is a qualified person with respect to electrical power transmission and distribution) is held to determine the procedures that will be followed to prevent electrical contact and electrocution.

    (4) *Insulating link/device.*

    (iv) Until November 8, 2011, the following procedure may be substituted for the requirements in paragraph ___ of this section: All employees, excluding equipment operators located on the equipment, who may come in contact with the equipment load line, or the load must be insulated or guarded from the equipment, the load line, and ___. Insulating ___ rated for the voltage involved are adequate insulation for the purposes of this paragraph.

    (a) (d)(3), the lift, pads
    (b) (d)(4), the hoisting equipment, mittens
    (c) (d)(4)(i), the load, gloves
    (d) (d)(4)(ii), the hosting equipment and accessories, pads

    Answer: (c) (d)(4)(i), the load, gloves. §1926.1410 (d)(4)(iv) Power line safety (all voltages). Subpart CC.

§1926.1410 (d)(4)(v) Power line safety (all voltages).
24. Equipment operations in which any part of the equipment, load line, or load (including rigging and lifting accessories) is closer than the minimum approach distance under Table A of §1926.1408 to an energized power line is prohibited, except where the employer demonstrates that all of the following requirements are met:

    (d) A planning meeting with the employer and the utility owner/operator (or registered professional engineer who is a qualified person with respect to electrical power transmission and distribution) is held to determine the procedures that will be followed to prevent electrical contact and electrocution.

    (4) *Insulating link/device.*

    (v) Until November 8, ___, the following procedure may be substituted for the requirement in (d)(4)(i) of this section:

    (a) 2010
    (b) 2011
    (c) 2012
    (d) 2013

    Answer: (d) 2013. §1926.1410 (d)(4)(v) Power line safety (all voltages). Subpart CC.

Subpart CC

§1926.1410 (d)(4)(v)(A) Power line safety (all voltages).
25. Equipment operations in which any part of the equipment, load line, or load (including rigging and lifting accessories) is closer than the minimum approach distance under Table A of §1926.1408 to an energized power line is prohibited, except where the employer demonstrates that all of the following requirements are met:
(d) A planning meeting with the employer and the utility owner/operator (or registered professional engineer who is a qualified person with respect to electrical power transmission and distribution) is held to determine the procedures that will be followed to prevent electrical contact and electrocution.
(4) *Insulating link/device.*
(v)(A) The employer must use a link/device manufactured on or before November 8, ___, that meets the definition of an insulating link/device, except that it has not been approved by a nationally Recognized Testing Laboratory, and that is maintained and used in accordance with manufacturer requirements and recommendations, and is installed at a point between the end of the load line (or below) and the load; and
(a) 2010
(b) 2011
(c) 2012
(d) 2013
Answer: (b) 2011. §1926.1410 (d)(4)(v)(A) Power line safety (all voltages). Subpart CC.

§1926.1410 (d)(4)(v)(B) Power line safety (all voltages).
26. Equipment operations in which any part of the equipment, load line, or load (including rigging and lifting accessories) is closer than the minimum approach distance under Table A of §1926.1408 to an energized power line is prohibited, except where the employer demonstrates that all of the following requirements are met:
(d) A planning meeting with the employer and the utility owner/operator (or registered professional engineer who is a qualified person with respect to electrical power transmission and distribution) is held to determine the procedures that will be followed to prevent electrical contact and electrocution.
(4) *Insulating link/device.*
(v)(B) All employees, excluding equipment operators located on the equipment, who may come in contact with the equipment, the load line, or the load must be insulated or ___ from the equipment, the load line, and the load through an additional means other than the device described in paragraph (d)(4)(v)(A) of this section.
(a) protected
(b) separated
(c) guarded
(d) positioned away
Answer: (c) guarded. §1926.1410 (d)(4)(v)(B) Power line safety (all voltages). Subpart CC.

Subpart CC

§1926.1410 (d)(4)(v)(B) Power line safety (all voltages).

27. Equipment operations in which any part of the equipment, load line, or load (including rigging and lifting accessories) is closer than the minimum approach distance under Table A of §1926.1408 to an energized power line is prohibited, except where the employer demonstrates that all of the following requirements are met:

(d) A planning meeting with the employer and the utility owner/operator (or registered professional engineer who is a qualified person with respect to electrical power transmission and distribution) is held to determine the procedures that will be followed to prevent electrical contact and electrocution.

(4) *Insulating link/device.*

(v)(B) All employees, excluding equipment operators located on the equipment, who may come in contact with the equipment, the load line, or the load must be insulated or ___ from the equipment, the load line, and the load through an additional means other than the device described in paragraph (d)(4)(v)(A) of this section. Insulating ___ rated for the voltage involved are adequate additional means of protection for the purposes of this paragraph.

(a) protected, sleeves
(b) separated, mittens
(c) guarded, gloves
(d) positioned away, pads

Answer: (c) guarded, gloves. §1926.1410 (d)(4)(v)(B) Power line safety (all voltages). Subpart CC.

§1926.1410 (d)(5) Power line safety (all voltages).

28. Equipment operations in which any part of the equipment, load line, or load (including rigging and lifting accessories) is closer than the minimum approach distance under Table A of §1926.1408 to an energized power line is prohibited, except where the employer demonstrates that all of the following requirements are met:

(d) A planning meeting with the employer and the utility owner/operator (or registered professional engineer who is a qualified person with respect to electrical power transmission and distribution) is held to determine the procedures that will be followed to prevent electrical contact and electrocution.

(5) Nonconductive rigging if the rigging may be within the Table ___ of §1926.1408 distance during the operation.

(a) 3
(b) A
(c) 5
(d) C

Answer: (b) A. §1926.1410 (d)(5) Power line safety (all voltages). Subpart CC.

Subpart CC

§1926.1410 (d)(6) Power line safety (all voltages).

29. Equipment operations in which any part of the equipment, load line, or load (including rigging and lifting accessories) is closer than the minimum approach distance under Table A of §1926.1408 to an energized power line is prohibited, except where the employer demonstrates that all of the following requirements are met:

(d) A planning meeting with the employer and the utility owner/operator (or registered professional engineer who is a qualified person with respect to electrical power transmission and distribution) is held to determine the procedures that will be followed to prevent electrical contact and electrocution.

(6) If the equipment is equipped with a device that automatically limits the range of movement, it ___ be used and set to prevent any part of the equipment, load line, or load (including rigging and lifting accessories) from ___ the minimum approach distance established under Paragraph (c) of this section.

(a) encroachment of
(b) encroaching
(c) breaching
(d) intruding into

Answer: (c) breaching. §1926.1410 (d)(6) Power line safety (all voltages). Subpart CC.

§1926.1410 (d)(7) Power line safety (all voltages).

30. Equipment operations in which any part of the equipment, load line, or load (including rigging and lifting accessories) is closer than the minimum approach distance under Table A of §1926.1408 to an energized power line is prohibited, except where the employer demonstrates that all of the following requirements are met:

(d) A planning meeting with the employer and the utility owner/operator (or registered professional engineer who is a qualified person with respect to electrical power transmission and distribution) is held to determine the procedures that will be followed to prevent electrical contact and electrocution.

(7) If a tag line is used, it must be of the nonconductive ___.

(a) Manila line
(b) design
(c) material
(d) type

Answer: (d) type. §1926.1410 (d)(7) Power line safety (all voltages). Subpart CC.

Subpart CC

§1926.1410 (d)(8) Power line safety (all voltages).

31. Equipment operations in which any part of the equipment, load line, or load (including rigging and lifting accessories) is closer than the minimum approach distance under Table A of §1926.1408 to an energized power line is prohibited, except where the employer demonstrates that all of the following requirements are met:
(d) A planning meeting with the employer and the utility owner/operator (or registered professional engineer who is a qualified person with respect to electrical power transmission and distribution) is held to determine the procedures that will be followed to prevent electrical contact and electrocution.
(8) Barricades forming a perimeter at least ___ feet away from the equipment to prevent unauthorized personnel from entering the work area.
(a)   10
(b)   12
(c)   15
(d)   18
Answer: (a) 10. §1926.1410 (d)(8) Power line safety (all voltages).
Subpart CC.

§1926.1410 (d)(8) Power line safety (all voltages).

32. Equipment operations in which any part of the equipment, load line, or load (including rigging and lifting accessories) is closer than the minimum approach distance under Table A of §1926.1408 to an energized power line is prohibited, except where the employer demonstrates that all of the following requirements are met:
(d) A planning meeting with the employer and the utility owner/operator (or registered professional engineer who is a qualified person with respect to electrical power transmission and distribution) is held to determine the procedures that will be followed to prevent electrical contact and electrocution.
(8) Barricades forming a perimeter at least ___ feet away from the equipment to prevent unauthorized personnel from entering the work area. In areas where obstacles prevent the barricade from being at least ___ feet away, the barricade must be as far from the equipment as feasible.
(a)   10, 10
(b)   12, 12
(c)   15, 15
(d)   18, 18
Answer: (a) 10, 10. §1926.1410 (d)(8) Power line safety (all voltages).
Subpart CC.

Subpart CC

§1926.1410 (d)(9) Power line safety (all voltages).
33. Equipment operations in which any part of the equipment, load line, or load (including rigging and lifting accessories) is closer than the minimum approach distance under Table A of §1926.1408 to an energized power line is prohibited, except where the employer demonstrates that all of the following requirements are met:
(d) A planning meeting with the employer and the utility owner/operator (or registered professional engineer who is a qualified person with respect to electrical power transmission and distribution) is held to determine the procedures that will be followed to prevent electrical contact and electrocution.
(9) Workers other than the operator must be ___ from touching the load line above the insulating link/device and crane.
(a) prevented
(b) cautioned
(c) warned
(d) prohibited
Answer: (d) prohibited. §1926.1410 (d)(9) Power line safety (all voltages).
Subpart CC.

§1926.1410 (d)(9) Power line safety (all voltages).
34. Equipment operations in which any part of the equipment, load line, or load (including rigging and lifting accessories) is closer than the minimum approach distance under Table A of §1926.1408 to an energized power line is prohibited, except where the employer demonstrates that all of the following requirements are met:
(d) A planning meeting with the employer and the utility owner/operator (or registered professional engineer who is a qualified person with respect to electrical power transmission and distribution) is held to determine the procedures that will be followed to prevent electrical contact and electrocution.
(9) Workers other than the operator must be ___ from touching the load line above the insulating link/device and crane. Operators remotely operating the equipment from the ground ___ use either wireless controls that isolate the operator from the equipment or insulating mats that insulate the operator from the ground.
(a) prevented, shall
(b) cautioned, shall
(c) warned, should
(d) prohibited, must
Answer: (d) prohibited, must. §1926.1410 (d)(9) Power line safety (all voltages).
Subpart CC.

Subpart CC

§1926.1410 (d)(10) Power line safety (all voltages).

35. Equipment operations in which any part of the equipment, load line, or load (including rigging and lifting accessories) is closer than the minimum approach distance under Table A of §1926.1408 to an energized power line is prohibited, except where the employer demonstrates that all of the following requirements are met:

(d) A planning meeting with the employer and the utility owner/operator (or registered professional engineer who is a qualified person with respect to electrical power transmission and distribution) is held to determine the procedures that will be followed to prevent electrical contact and electrocution.

(10) Only personnel ___ to the operation are permitted to be in the area of the crane and load.

(a) essential
(b) assigned
(c) required
(d) assisting

Answer: (a) essential. §1926.1410 (d)(10) Power line safety (all voltages). Subpart CC.

§1926.1410 (d)(11) Power line safety (all voltages).

36. Equipment operations in which any part of the equipment, load line, or load (including rigging and lifting accessories) is closer than the minimum approach distance under Table A of §1926.1408 to an energized power line is prohibited, except where the employer demonstrates that all of the following requirements are met:

(d) A planning meeting with the employer and the utility owner/operator (or registered professional engineer who is a qualified person with respect to electrical power transmission and distribution) is held to determine the procedures that will be followed to prevent electrical contact and electrocution.

(11) The equipment ___ be properly grounded.

(a) shall
(b) must
(c) will
(d) is to

Answer: (b) must. §1926.1410 (d)(11) Power line safety (all voltages). Subpart CC.

Subpart CC

§1926.1410 (d)(12) Power line safety (all voltages).
37. Equipment operations in which any part of the equipment, load line, or load (including rigging and lifting accessories) is closer than the minimum approach distance under Table A of §1926.1408 to an energized power line is prohibited, except where the employer demonstrates that all of the following requirements are met:
(d) A planning meeting with the employer and the utility owner/operator (or registered professional engineer who is a qualified person with respect to electrical power transmission and distribution) is held to determine the procedures that will be followed to prevent electrical contact and electrocution.
(12) Insulating line hose or ___ must be installed by the utility owner/operator except where such devices are unavailable for the line voltage involved.
 (a) protective covers
 (b) protective cover
 (c) cover-up
 (d) line shielding
Answer: (b) must. §1926.1410 (d)(12) Power line safety (all voltages). Subpart CC.

§1926.1410 (e) Power line safety (all voltages).
38. Equipment operations in which any part of the equipment, load line, or load (including rigging and lifting accessories) is closer than the minimum approach distance under Table A of §1926.1408 to an energized power line is prohibited, except where the employer demonstrates that all of the following requirements are met:
(e) The procedures ___ to comply with paragraph (d) of this section are documented and immediately available on-site.
 (a) approved
 (b) required
 (c) developed
 (d) necessary
Answer: (c) developed. §1926.1410 (e) Power line safety (all voltages). Subpart CC.

§1926.1410 (f) Power line safety (all voltages).
39. Equipment operations in which any part of the equipment, load line, or load (including rigging and lifting accessories) is closer than the minimum approach distance under Table A of §1926.1408 to an energized power line is prohibited, except where the employer demonstrates that all of the following requirements are met:
(f) The equipment user and utility owner/operator (or registered professional engineer) meet with the equipment operator and the other workers who will be in the area of the equipment or load to review the procedures that will be ___ to prevent breaching the minimum approach distance established in paragraph (c) of this section and prevent electrocution.
 (a) mandated
 (b) enforced
 (c) mandatory
 (d) implemented
Answer: (d) implemented. §1926.1410 (f) Power line safety (all voltages). Subpart CC.

Subpart CC

§1926.1410 (g) Power line safety (all voltages).
40. Equipment operations in which any part of the equipment, load line, or load (including rigging and lifting accessories) is closer than the minimum approach distance under Table A of §1926.1408 to an energized power line is prohibited, except where the employer demonstrates that all of the following requirements are met:
(g) The procedures developed to comply with paragraph ___ of this section are implemented.
(a) (a)
(b) (b)
(c) (c)
(d) (d)
Answer: (d) (d). §1926.1410 (g) Power line safety (all voltages).
Subpart CC.

§1926.1410 (h) Power line safety (all voltages).
41. Equipment operations in which any part of the equipment, load line, or load (including rigging and lifting accessories) is closer than the minimum approach distance under Table A of §1926.1408 to an energized power line is prohibited, except where the employer demonstrates that all of the following requirements are met:
(h) The utility owner/operator (or registered professional engineer) and all employers of employees involved in the work must identify ___ who will direct the implementation of the procedures.
(a) a person
(b) an individual
(c) one person
(d) one supervisor
Answer: (c) one person. §1926.1410 (h) Power line safety (all voltages).
Subpart CC.

§1926.1410 (h) Power line safety (all voltages).
42. Equipment operations in which any part of the equipment, load line, or load (including rigging and lifting accessories) is closer than the minimum approach distance under Table A of §1926.1408 to an energized power line is prohibited, except where the employer demonstrates that all of the following requirements are met:
(h) The utility owner/operator (or registered professional engineer) and all employers of employees involved in the work must identify ___ who will direct the implementation of the procedures. The person identified in accordance with this paragraph must direct the implementation of the procedures and must have the authority to ___ at any time to ensure safety.
(a) stop work
(b) stop the work
(c) stop the job
(d) require and enforce immediate corrections
Answer: (a) stop work. §1926.1410 (h) Power line safety (all voltages).
Subpart CC.

Subpart CC

(i) [Reserved]

§1926.1410 (j) Power line safety (all voltages).
43. Equipment operations in which any part of the equipment, load line, or load (including rigging and lifting accessories) is closer than the minimum approach distance under Table A of §1926.1408 to an energized power line is prohibited, except where the employer demonstrates that all of the following requirements are met:
(j) If a problem occurs implementing the procedures being used to comply with paragraph (d) of this section, or indicating that those procedures are ___ to prevent electrocution, the employer must safely stop operations and either develop new procedures to comply with paragraph (d) of this section or have the utility owner/operator deenergize and visibly ground or relocate the power line before resuming work.
 (a) out dated
 (b) insufficient
 (c) inadequate
 (d) obsolete
Answer: (b) insufficient. §1926.1410 (j) Power line safety (all voltages).
Subpart CC.

§1926.1410 (k) Power line safety (all voltages).
44. Equipment operations in which any part of the equipment, load line, or load (including rigging and lifting accessories) is closer than the minimum approach distance under Table A of §1926.1408 to an energized power line is prohibited, except where the employer demonstrates that all of the following requirements are met:
(k) Devices originally designed by the manufacturer for use as a safety device (see §1926.1415), operational aid, or means to prevent power line contact or electrocution, when used to comply with this section, ___ comply with the manufacturer's procedures for use and conditions of use.
 (a) shall
 (b) must
 (c) may
 (d) must always
Answer: (b) must. §1926.1410 (k) Power line safety (all voltages).
Subpart CC.

(l) [Reserved]

Subpart CC

§1926.1410 (m) Power line safety (all voltages).
45. Equipment operations in which any part of the equipment, load line, or load (including rigging and lifting accessories) is closer than the minimum approach distance under Table A of §1926.1408 to an energized power line is prohibited, except where the employer demonstrates that all of the following requirements are met:
(m) The employer must train each operator and crew member assigned to work with the equipment in accordance with §___.
   (a)   1926. 1408 (g)
   (b)   1926.1408 (h)
   (c)   1926.1408 (i)
   (d)   1926.1408(j)
Answer: (a)1926.1408 (g). §1926.1410 (m) Power line safety (all voltages). Subpart CC.

A Ficus Tree Publishing LLC. Quick Notes Page

DU VALLS
OSHA 1926 Subpart CC — Cranes and Derricks in Construction
OSHA 1926.1411 Power line safety—
While traveling under or near power lines with no load.
Instructors Manual 2014 Edition
OSHA Test CC - 15

§1926.1411 Power line safety—while traveling under or near power lines with no load.
1. (a) This section establishes procedures and criteria that must be met for equipment traveling under or near a power line on a ___ with no load.
    (a) highway
    (b) roadway
    (c) job site
    (d) construction site
    Answer: (d) construction site. §1926.1410 Power line safety (all voltages). Subpart CC.

§1926.1411 Power line safety—while traveling under or near power lines with no load.
2. (a) This section establishes procedures and criteria that must be met for equipment traveling under or near a power line on a ___ with no load. Equipment traveling on a construction site with a load is governed by §§1926.1408, 1926.1409 or ___, whichever is appropriate, and
    (a) highway, 1910.563
    (b) roadway, 1926.560
    (c) job site, 1926.555
    (d) construction site, 1926.1410
    Answer: (d) construction site, 1926.1410. §1926.1410 Power line safety (all voltages). Subpart CC.

§1926.1411 Power line safety—while traveling under or near power lines with no load.
3. (a) This section establishes procedures and criteria that must be met for equipment traveling under or near a power line on a ___ with no load. Equipment traveling on a construction site with a load is governed by §§1926.1408, 1926.1409 or ___, whichever is appropriate, and §___.
    (a) highway, 1910.563, 1926.1417(k)
    (b) roadway, 1926.560, 1926.1417(m)
    (c) job site, 1926.555, 1926.1417(v)
    (d) construction site, 1926.1410, 1926.1417(u)
    Answer: (d) construction site, 1926.1410, 1926.1417(u). §1926.1410 Power line safety (all voltages). Subpart CC.

Subpart CC

§1926.1411 (b) Power line safety—while traveling under or near power lines with no load.
4.   (b) The employer must ensure that:
(1) The boom/mast and boom/mast support system are lowered ___ to meet the requirements of this paragraph.
- (a)   adequately
- (b)   sufficiently
- (c)   completely
- (d)   according to regulations

Answer: (b) sufficiently. §1926.1410 Power line safety— while traveling. Subpart CC.

§1926.1411 (b) Power line safety—while traveling under or near power lines with no load.
5.   (b) The employer must ensure that:
(1) The boom/mast and boom/mast support system are lowered ___ to meet the requirements of this paragraph.
(2) The clearances specified in Table T of this section are ___.
- (a)   adequately, followed
- (b)   sufficiently, maintained
- (c)   completely, enforced
- (d)   according to regulations, followed

Answer: (b) sufficiently, maintained. §1926.1410 Power line safety— while traveling. Subpart CC.

§1926.1411 (b) Power line safety—while traveling under or near power lines with no load.
6.   (b) The employer must ensure that:
(1) The boom/mast and boom/mast support system are lowered ___ to meet the requirements of this paragraph.
(2) The clearances specified in Table T of this section are ___.
(3) The effects of speed and terrain on equipment (including movement of the boom/mast are considered so that those effects do not cause the minimum clearance distances specified in Table T of this section to be ___.
- (a)   adequately, followed, ignored
- (b)   sufficiently, maintained, breached
- (c)   completely, enforced, compromised
- (d)   according to regulations, followed,

Answer: (b) sufficiently, maintained, breached. §1926.1410 Power line safety— while traveling. Subpart CC.

Subpart CC

§1926.1411 (b) Power line safety—while traveling under or near power lines with no load.

7. (b) The employer must ensure that:
    (4) *Dedicated spotter*. If any part of the equipment while traveling will get closer than ___ feet to the power line, the employer must ensure that a dedicated spotter who is is in continuous contact with the driver/operator is used. The dedicated spotter must:
    (a) 10
    (b) 15
    (c) 20
    (d) 25
    Answer: (c) 20. §1926.1410 (b)(4). Power line safety— while traveling. Subpart CC.

§1926.1411 (b)(4)(i) Power line safety—while traveling under or near power lines with no load.

8. (b) The employer must ensure that:
    (4)(i) *Dedicated spotter*. If any part of the equipment while traveling will get closer than ___ feet to the power line, the employer must ensure that a dedicated spotter who is is in continuous contact with the driver/operator is used. The dedicated spotter must:
    (i) Be positioned to ___ gauge the clearance distance.
    (a) 10, absolutely
    (b) 15, efficiently
    (c) 20, effectively
    (d) 25, accurately
    Answer: (c) 20, effectively. §1926.1410 (b)(4). Power line safety— while traveling. Subpart CC.

§1926.1411 (b)(4)(i), (ii) Power line safety—while traveling under or near power lines with no load.

9. (b)(4)(i), (ii) The employer must ensure that:
    (4) *Dedicated spotter*. If any part of the equipment while traveling will get closer than ___ feet to the power line, the employer must ensure that a dedicated spotter who is is in continuous contact with the driver/operator is used. The dedicated spotter must:
    (i) Be positioned to ___ gauge the clearance distance.
    (ii) Where necessary, use equipment that ___ the dedicated spotter to communicate directly with the operator.
    (a) 10, absolutely, allows
    (b) 15, efficiently, enables
    (c) 20, effectively, provides
    (d) 25, accurately, permits
    Answer: (c) 20, effectively, enables. §1926.1410 (b)(4)(i), (ii). Power line safety— while traveling. Subpart CC.

Subpart CC

§1926.1411 (b)(4)(ii), (iii) Power line safety—while traveling under or near power lines with no load.

10. (b)(4)(i), (ii), (iii) The employer must ensure that:
(4) *Dedicated spotter*. If any part of the equipment while traveling will get closer than ___feet to the power line, the employer must ensure that a dedicated spotter who is is in continuous contact with the driver/operator is used. The dedicated spotter must:
(i) Be positioned to ___ gauge the clearance distance.
(ii) Where necessary, use equipment that ___ the dedicated spotter to communicate directly with the operator.
(iii) Give timely information to the operator so that the required clearance distance can be ___.

(a) 10, absolutely, allows, met
(b) 15, efficiently, enables, maintained
(c) 20, effectively, provides, met
(d) 25, accurately, permits, maintained

Answer: (c) 20, effectively, enables, maintained. §1926.1410 (b)(4)(ii), (iii). Power line safety—while traveling. Subpart CC.

§1926.1411 (b)(5) Power line safety—while traveling under or near power lines with no load.

11. (b)(5) The employer must ensure that:
(5) Additional precautions for traveling in ___visibility.

(a) poor
(b) limited
(c) hazardous
(d) inclement

Answer: (a) poor. §1926.1410 (b)(5). Power line safety—while traveling. Subpart CC.

§1926.1411 (b)(5) Power line safety—while traveling under or near power lines with no load.

12. (b)(5) The employer must ensure that:
(5) Additional precautions for traveling in ___visibility. When traveling at night, or in conditions of poor visibility, in addition to the ___ specified in paragraphs (b)(1) through (___) of this section, the employer must

(a) poor, (4)
(b) limited, (4)(i)
(c) hazardous, (4)(ii)
(d) inclement, (4)(iii)

Answer: (a) poor, (4). §1926.1410 (b)(5). Power line safety—while traveling. Subpart CC.

Subpart CC

§1926.1411 (b)(5) Power line safety—while traveling under or near power lines with no load.
13. (b)(5) The employer must ensure that:
(5) Additional precautions for traveling in ___ visibility. When traveling at night, or in conditions of poor visibility, in addition to the ___ specified in paragraphs (b)(1) through (__) of this section, the employer must ensure that :
(i) The power line are ___ or another means of identifying the location of the lines is used.
(a)   poor, (4), illuminated
(b)   limited, (4)(i), marked
(c)   hazardous, (4)(ii), identified
(d)   inclement, (4)(iii), clearly located
Answer: (a) poor, (4), illuminated. §1926.1410 (b)(5)(i). Power line safety—while traveling. Subpart CC.

§1926.1411 (b)(5) Power line safety—while traveling under or near power lines with no load.
14. (b)(5) The employer must ensure that:
(5) Additional precautions for traveling in ___ visibility. When traveling at night, or in conditions of poor visibility, in addition to the ___ specified in paragraphs (b)(1) through (__) of this section, the employer must ensure that :
(i) The power line are ___ or another means of identifying the location of the lines is used.
(ii) A safe path of travel is ___ and used.
(a)   poor, (4), illuminated, identified
(b)   limited, (4)(i), marked, determined
(c)   hazardous, (4)(ii), identified
(d)   inclement, (4)(iii), clearly located
Answer: (a) poor, (4), illuminated, identified. §1926.1410 (b)(5)(i), (ii). Power line safety—while traveling. Subpart CC.

Table T—Minimum Clearance Distances While Traveling With No Load
Voltage (nominal, kV, alternating current) while traveling—minimum clearance distance (feet)

15. Up to 0.75
(a)   3
(b)   4
(c)   5
(d)   6
Answer: (b) 4. feet. Table T

16. Over .75 to 50
(a)   3
(b)   4
(c)   5
(d)   6
Answer: (d) 6 feet. Table T

Table T—Minimum Clearance Distances While Traveling With No Load

Voltage (nominal, kV, alternating current) while traveling—minimum clearance distance (feet)

17. Over 50 to 345
    (a) 6
    (b) 10
    (c) 16
    (d) 20
    Answer: (b) 10 feet. Table T

18. Over 345 to 750
    (a) 6
    (b) 10
    (c) 16
    (d) 20
    Answer: (c) 16 feet. Table T

19. Over 750 to 1,000
    (a) 6
    (b) 10
    (c) 16
    (d) 20
    Answer: (d) 20 feet. Table T

20. Over 1,000 — (as ___ by the utility owner/operator or registered professional engineer who is a qualified person with respect to electrical power transmission and distribution).
    (a) required
    (b) established
    (c) State statutes
    (d) Federal regulations
    Answer: (b) established. Table T—Minimum clearance distances while traveling with no load.

Ficus Tree Publishing LLC. Instructors Manuals

Amazon   Create Space   Kindle

OSHA Publications for 2014
Instructors Manual 2014 Edition of OSHA
1903
1904
1910
1926

The above listed DUVALLS OSHA Instructors Manuals, 2014 Edition are now available from Amazon.com, in soft cover print-on-demand (P.O.D.) format. The copyrighted works are also available from Kindle and the e-book version from Amazon's Create Space. Professors, Teachers, and Instructors will be notified as our additional Master Study Guide Series become available via the above listed sources.

The Works, our publications, are comprehensive Instructors Manuals with multiple-choice questions set forth generally, in direct sequence to the official Department of Labor, U.S. government publication. The multiple-choice questions with answers provide a simplified easy to read, easy to study platform for your students and for you, the instructor to develop your course material.

The Instructors Manuals are designed as the textbook material for each specific course required for your lecture series. With very little effort you, the Instructor, have at your fingertips the necessary comprehensive class syllabus material for each new scholastic quarter or semester without the accompanying, unnecessary, workload stress.

The work is presented in a generally sequential format that faithfully parallels the official United States Publications. Further, there are no intentional "trick" questions. There are difficult questions for your students to solve but all questions are provided with answers. It is a simple process for your students to follow. Read the sentence, paragraph or passage as written in the text then read and solve the test question. The initial lecture, the reading of the text and the solving of the problem reinforces the basic learning processes.

It is a simple, easy and efficient procedure.

© Copyright 2014. All rights reserved. Warning: United States Copyright Law and International Treaties prohibit unauthorized publication, distribution and reproduction of the whole, part, portion of this Work. Unauthorized use of this copyright in any form, format, sequence or document may result in severe criminal and civil penalties. Violations of this copyright are investigated by the United States Department of Justice and carry, upon conviction of fines up to $250,000 and five years confinement.
A Ficus Tree Publishing LLC., Educational - Technical Publication

29 CFR OSHA

Part 1903
Inspections, Citations and Proposed Penalties

OSHA Part 1903 provides information to the rules and requirements for Inspections, Citations and Proposed Penalties. This Instructors Manual for 2014 contains approximately 145 pages of information, text, and multiple-choice test type questions. Over 300 questions with answers.

Information provided in the form of multiple-choice test type questions with answers is progressive, generally sequential to the official Part 1903 publication. Information presented relates to the following" Williams-Steiger Act. the General Duty Clause. The conduct of inspections. General enforcement policy. Posting of a notice. Dimensions of posters. Reproductions of posters. Availability of the Act. Authority for inspection. Objection to inspection. Entry not a waiver. Advance notice of inspections. Conduct of inspections.

This work is a Instructors Manual created specifically for OSHA 1903. The intent is to reduce a level of pressure caused by searching documents and records for suitable lecture material.

Part 1904
Recording and Reporting Illnesses and Injuries

OSHA Part 1904 is an important publication for all businesses. As an employer you are responsible. the Instructors Manual contains 208 pages with over 500 questions, soft cover, printed in black and white. Generally sequential test type, multiple-choice questions provided with answers, parallel the official OSHA publication. The multiple-choice questions includes but not limited to the following standards: §1904.1 Subpart A—Purpose. §1904.1Subpart B—Scope. §1904.2 Partial exemption for employers with 10 or fewer employees. §1904.2 Partial exemption for certain industries. §1904.3 Keeping records for more than one agency. §1904 Subpart B App A— Partially Exempt Industries SIC codes. The Decision Tree. §1904.4 Subpart C—Recording criteria. §1904.5 Determination of work-relatedness. §1904.6 Determination of new cases. §1904.7 Subpart C—General recording criteria. §1904.8 —Needlestick and sharps injuries. §1904.9 Recording criteria for cases involving medical removal under OSHA standards. §1904.10—Recording criteria involving hearing loss. §1904.11—Recording criteria for work-related tuberculosis cases. §1904.29 Forms. §1904.30 Multiple business establishments. §1904.31 — Covered employees. §1904.32 Annual summary. §1904.33 Retention and updating, (important - how long must you retain the records)? §1904.34 Change in business ownership. §1904.35 Employee involvement. §1904.36 Prohibition against discrimination. §1904.37 State recordkeeping regulations. §1904.38 Variances from the recordkeeping. §1904.39 reporting fatalities and multiple hospitalization incidents to OSHA. §1904.40 Providing records to government representatives. §1904.41 Annual OSHA injury and illness survey of ten or more employers. §1904.42 Requests from the Bureau of Labor Statistics for data. §1904.43 Summary and posting of 2001 data. §1904.44 Retention and updating of old forms. §1904.45 OMB control numbers under the Paperwork Reduction Act. §1904.46 Definitions.

29 CFR OSHA

Part 1910 Occupational Safety and Health Standards (The Subparts)

Part 1926
Safety and Health Regulations For Construction (The Subparts)

§1926 Subpart A—General

70 pages. A soft cover, fastback binding, printed black and white. Over 100 test type multiple-choice questions with answers written in general sequential format that parallels the official Department of Labor publication. Subpart test questions include the following: §1926.1 Purpose and scope. §1926.2 Variances from safety and health standards. §1926.3 Inspections - right of entry. §1926.4 Rules of practice for administrative adjudications for enforcement of safety and health standards. §1926.5 OMB control numbers test questions with answers. §1926.6 Incorporation by reference. Both §§ 1926.5 and 1926.6 are frequently overlooked when studying for professional tests. However, questions from this part do appear on professional and licensing examination with greater frequency.

§1926 Subpart B—General Interpretations

OSHA 1926 Subpart B—General Interpretations Instructors Manual 2014 Edition, provides within approximately 102 pages a series of fifteen (15) tests that provide an estimated 275 + multiple-choice, test type questions with answers.

The tests are designed to enable the Instructor to focus on the development of the course Semester, Quarter syllabus by providing complete and up to date information on each specific subpart of 29 CFR OSHA Part 1926. Each of the test series generally follow the exacting published format provided by the Department of Labor in electronic and hard copy editions of the stated Part. The detailed work available to Instructors includes questions with answers for the following:

§1926.10 Scope of subpart. §1926.11 Coverage under section 103 of the act distinguished (for both (a) and (b)). The very important §1926.12 Reorganization Plan No. 14 of 1950. (a) General provisions including all (58) paragraphs. §1926.13 Interpretation of statutory terms (a, b, and c). §1926.15 Relationship to the Service Contract Act; Walsh-Healey Public Contracts Act (a and b). §1926.16 Rules of construction. (the Prime Contractor, Subcontractor and Subcontractors).

Authority: Sec. 107, Contract Work Hours and Safety Standards Act (Construction Safety Act) (40 U.S.C 333). Subpart B of this part provides statements and information of general policy and interpretations of section 107 of the Contract Work Hours and Safety Standards Act having general applicability. (b) *The Plan*. (1) addresses include the a specific section of the CFR's - The Code of Federal Regulations.

§1926 Subpart C—General Safety and Health Provisions

OSHA 1926 Subpart C—General Safety and Health Provisions Instructors Manual 2014 Edition, provides 60+ pages of text and over 170 multiple-choice, test type questions with answers.

Description:
The tests are designed to enable Instructors and lecturers to focus on the development of the course Semester, Quarter syllabus by providing complete and up to date information for and of Part 1926 Subpart C—General Safety and Health Provisions. Each test series will generally follow the exacting published format of the standards provided by the Department of Labor in electronic and hard copy editions of the stated OSHA Part. This detailed work available to Instructors includes questions with answers for the following:

The Authority for Sec. 3704, Contract Work Hours and Safety Standards Act is stated by initiating this multiple-choice series the first test question with the answer followed immediately by multiple-choice questions pertaining to §1926.20 in sequence to the Department of Labor publication. This first series of multiple-choice test questions with answers provides over twenty questions with answers for §1926.20.

§1926.21 Safety training and education (another 20 plus multiple-choice questions) is followed by the brief notice §1926.22 is reserved. §1926.23 First aid and medical attention provided by OSHA is a single sentence statement referencing to subpart D of this part. Note that while only two multiple-choice test type questions were created from the single OSHA sentence. The purpose of providing this separate identification for §1926.23 is to parallel (without changing or merging) the Department of Labor publication for the information provided with §1926.23. A similar procedure is followed for §1926.24 Fire protection and prevention where the paragraph provides basic information related to the content of §1926.24 Fire protection and prevention while referencing to subpart F of this part.

§1926 Subpart —C multiple-choice questions continue with §1926.25 Housekeeping (keeping the job site clean and safe); §1926.26 Illumination with reference to subpart D of this part.; §1926.27 Sanitation with reference to subpart D of this part; §1926.28 Personal protective equipment; §1926.29 Acceptable certifications; §1926.30 Shipbuilding and ship repairing; §1926.32 Definitions; §1926.33 Access to employee exposure and medical records; §1926.34 Means of egress; concluding with OSHA §1926.35 Employee emergency action plans and the FR information.

§1926 Subpart D—Occupational Health and Environmental Controls

OSHA 1926 Subpart D—Occupational Health and Environmental Controls Instructors Manual 2014 Edition, provides 60+ pages of text and over 170 multiple-choice, test type questions with answers**.**

Description:
The tests are designed to enable Instructors and lecturers to focus on the development of the course Semester, Quarter syllabus by providing complete and up to date information for and of Part 1926 Subpart D—Occupational Health and Environmental Controls. This test series will generally follow the exacting published format of the standards provided by the Department of Labor in electronic and hard copy editions of the stated OSHA Part. This detailed work available to Instructors includes questions with answers for the following:

The Authority for Sec. 3704, Contract Work Hours and Safety Standards Act is stated by initiating this multiple-choice series the first test question with the answer followed immediately by multiple-choice questions pertaining to §1926.20 in sequence to the Department of Labor publication. This first series of multiple-choice test questions with answers provides over twenty questions with answers for §1926.20.

OSHA 1926 Subpart D—Occupational Health and Environmental Controls Instructors Manual 2014 Edition, provides 60+ pages of text and over 170 multiple-choice, test type questions with answers

Description

§1926.1400 Subpart CC—Cranes and Derricks in Construction

This publication provides information in the manner of multiple-choice questions with answers for OSHA §1926.1400 through and including OSHA §1926.1411 including Table T—Minimum Clearance Distances While Traveling With No Load.

DU VALLS OSHA 1926 CC — Cranes and Derricks in Construction. Instructors Manual 2014 Edition, Subpart CC

§1926.1400 Scope.
1. "(a) This standard applies to power-operated equipment, when used in construction, that can hoist, lower and horizontally move a suspended load. Such equipment includes, but is not limited to: Articulating cranes (such as knuckle-boom cranes); crawler cranes; floating cranes; cranes on barges; locomotive cranes; mobile cranes (such as wheel-mounted, rough-terrain, all-terrain, commercial truck-mounted, and boom truck cranes); multi-purpose machines when configured to hoist and lower (by means of a winch or hook) and horizontally move a suspended load; industrial cranes (such as carry-deck cranes); dedicated pile drivers; service/mechanic trucks with a hoisting device; a crane on a monorail; tower cranes (such as a fixed jib, *i.e.,* "hammerhead boom"), luffing boom and self-erecting); pedestal cranes; portal cranes; overhead gantry cranes; sideboom cranes; derricks; and variations of such equipment. However, items listed in paragraph (c) of this section are excluded from the scope of this standard."

The entire paragraph above is taken as a verbatim presentation from the lead-in paragraph for OSHA standard **§1926.1400 Subpart CC—Cranes and Derricks in Construction**. What we have accomplished with the creation of DUVALLS OSHA 1926 CC Instructors Manual 2014 Edition is the dissection of this entire statement into a series of multiple-choice test type questions presented in convenient, easy to read, easy to follow test type questions. All questions are provided with answers, all questions with their answers are written in the specific sequential format of the United States Department of Labor publication.

For convenience of study and research each work presented by Ficus Tree Publishing LLC., for OSHA is generally limited from 60 to 150 pages plus or minus.

The Instructor, the student, the researcher will generally encounter little difficulty when reading, studying, and researching the difficult Federal Laws, Rules and Regulations (CFR's) of our complex but very important OSHA—Occupational Safety and Health Act when presented in this modern method study format.

This work is printed and marketed through and by Amazon/Create Space. Soon to be available on Kindle.

January 2014 OSHA 1926 Base Data
Department of Labor

§1926 Subpart D—Occupational Health and Environmental Controls
(Written, under review and updating)

§1926 Subpart E—Personal Protective and Life Saving Equipment
(Written, under review and updating)

§1926 Subpart F—Fire Protection and Prevention
(Written, under review and updating)

§1926 Subpart G—Signs, Signals, and Barricades
(Written, under review and updating)

§1926 Subpart H—Materials Handling, Storage, Use, and Disposal
(Written, under review and updating)

§1926 Subpart I—Tools—Hand and Power
(Written, under review and updating)

§1926 Subpart J—Welding and Cutting
(Written, under review and updating)

§1926 Subpart K—Electrical
(Written, under review and updating)

§1926 Subpart L—Scaffolds
(Written, under review and updating)

§1926 Subpart M—Fall Protection
(Written, under review and updating)

§1926 Subpart N—Cranes, Derricks, Hoists, Elevators,
Conveyors and Helicopter Operations
(Written, under review and updating)

§1926 Subpart O—Motor Vehicles, Mechanized Equipment, and Marine Operations
(Written, under review and updating)

§1926 Subpart P—Excavations
(Written, under review and updating)

© Copyright 2014. All rights reserved. Warning: United States Copyright Law and International Treaties prohibit unauthorized publication, distribution and reproduction of the whole, part, portion of this Work. Unauthorized use of this copyright in any form, format, sequence or document may result in severe criminal and civil penalties. Violations of this copyright are investigated by the United States Department of Justice and carry, upon conviction of fines up to $250,000 and five years confinement.
A Ficus Tree Publishing LLC., Educational - Technical Publication

January 2014 OSHA 1926 Base Data
Department of Labor

§1926 Subpart Q—Concrete and Masonry Construction
(Written, under review and updating)

§1926 Subpart R—Steel Erection
(Written, under review and updating)

§1926 Subpart S—Underground Constructions, Caissons, Cofferdams and Compressed Air
(Written, under review and updating)

§1926 Subpart T—Demolition
(Written, under review and updating)

§1926 Subpart U—Blasting and the Use of Explosives
(Unavailable)

§1926 Subpart V—Power Transmission and Distribution
(Written, under review and updating)

§1926 Subpart W—Rollover Protective Structures, Overhead Protection
(Written, under review and updating)

§1926 Subpart X—Stairways and Ladders
(Written, under review and updating)

§1926 Subpart Y—Diving
(Written, under review and updating)

§1926 Subpart Z—Toxic and Hazardous Substances
(Written, under review and updating)

§1926 Subpart CC—Cranes and Derricks in Construction
(In progress)

Reminder:

Department of Labor Occupational Safety and Health Administration. 29 CFR Part 1926. [Docket No. OSHA-2007-0066] RIN No. 1218-AC61

Cranes and Derricks in Construction: Underground Construction and Demolition.

Agency: Occupational Safety and Health Administration (OSHA), Labor.

Action: Final rule.

SUMMARY: On August 17, 2012, OSHA issued a notice of proposed rulemaking, as well as a companion direct final rule, that proposed applying the requirements in OSHA's 2010 cranes and derricks construction standard to underground construction work and demolition work. The notice of proposed rulemaking also proposed to correct inadvertent errors in the underground construction and demolition standards. After receiving a comment recommending that OSHA clarify the proposed regulatory text of the demolition standard, OSHA clarified the text and is issuing this final rule to apply the cranes and derricks standard to underground construction work and demolition work.

Date: This final rule is effective May 23, 2013. Petitions for the final rule of this final review are due on June 24, 2013.

CPSIA information can be obtained
at www.ICGtesting.com
Printed in the USA
BVOW04s0750050417
480357BV00017B/104/P